Self Care

May God bless
you as you stay in
a fresh place.

Dr. Orme

Self Care

Through Prayer and Forgiveness

Dr. Helen Orme

To order additional copies of this book, contact:
Xlibris Corporation
1-888-795-4274
www.Xlibris.com
Orders@Xlibris.com
89705

CONTENTS

Acknowledgements

I would like to especially thank God for my family and for their support. A special thank you goes to my husband Tony. To my beautiful children Tasha, Dion, Michael, Brian, and grandchildren Victoria, Paris, Omar and Ameena, thank you for your encouragement as I worked to fulfill my dream. A special thank you to the awesome family at Shekinah Glory Tabernacle for your support and love. I greatly appreciate Dr. Jackie McCullough, Dr. Billie Ann Davis, Tasha Bentley, Shawni Jackson, Delores Brown, Robinlynne Lafayette, Jessica Williams, Kristine M. Smith and Virginia Pearson for their support and help during this project. Last but not least, a special thanks to the Destiny Learning and Leadership Center and the awe-inspiring Common Thread focus group.

Preface

The purpose of this project is to empower women leaders to engage in self-care through prayer and forgiveness. Take whatever time you need to minister prayer and forgiveness to yourself on an ongoing basic; doing so is crucial. If you'll do this daily, you'll remain fresh and vibrant when ministering to others. The practice fosters spiritual, emotional, and physical wholeness, and will stimulate personal integrity.

Embedded in our culture is the propensity to "serve" by caring and nurturing others, forsaking the self when given the opportunity to fulfill the Call. Female leaders take little time to care for themselves. For some, self-care is not a high priority on the Task for the Day List. Maintaining spiritual and physical stamina is just as important as keeping abreast of the liturgical duties of the day.

The two key components used in this project are prayer and forgiveness. Prayer is one of the vehicles God uses to talk to you. Forgiveness is one of His commandments. We routinely use both of these disciplines to nurture and minister to others. It's vital to use them when caring for yourself, too. Those who do, experience spiritual depth and wholeness because they are renewed in spirit every day and abide in a fresh place.

I've found these components to be key principles for women in leadership. You need to give yourself permission to listen to and honoring yourself, to attend to your physical and spiritual needs. Doing so frees you to engage in self-care, recover your waning energy and move forward with renewed vibrancy. It also liberates your ministry.

As I was growing up, I often visited my grandmother, taking the Greyhound bus from Illinois to her home in Missouri. She would tell me to put my money in a handkerchief and tie it in a knot, then pin it inside my bra with a safety pin—that way no one could take my money if I went to sleep on the bus. The knot was uncomfortable, but comfort was not important. The goal was to hide the money, so no one could take it while I was asleep.

Life can be like that. We take our past disappointments and pains, knot them inside a handkerchief, and tuck them away so no one can get to them. We don't deal with the stuff we have not taken the time to resolve; we tuck it away so we can attend to others.

We have to use a new set of lens. With self care, we get rid of the weight that so easily besets us. We give ourselves the opportunity to start in a fresh place as we travel to greater heights.

Traveling on the bus to my visit my grandmother can be viewed as parallel to our walk with Christ. We begin the journey with a handkerchief tucked neatly away so no one will know of our challenges or issues. Graciously, we think, we keep it tucked away so no one will take it. But hiding your own need to forgive and let go is uncomfortable.

Self care through prayer and forgiveness enables you to close the door on the past. It pushes you forward as you enter God's plan and purpose for your life. Applying the principles of prayer and forgiveness to yourself and others lets you recover your sense of self and enjoy true liberation. *"In meekness instructing those that oppose themselves; if God peradventure will give them repentance to the acknowledging of the truth; And that they may recover themselves . . . "* (2 Tim. 2:25-26 [NKJ]).

Forgiveness is an act of giving, an act of being compassionate with yourself. When you give, you turn control over to someone without cost or obligation (*New World Dictionary of American Language*). When you forgive, you give control of your destiny to God.

Freely pardoning yourself and others releases you to live life creatively again in the same way you lived prior to the injury or insult. The discipline of forgiveness allows God to take control. It also allows agape love to manifest within you for yourself and for others.

The ability to understand and express affection for yourself bestows a deep feeling of compassion and kindness in the midst of transitions. In granting yourself mercy, you allow God to heal your wounded, negative sense of self—the life-draining "I ought to" or "I should have" thoughts.

Permission and receiving are crucial components of forgiveness. Giving yourself **permission** to receive or accept forgiveness is paramount. Opening your heart to receive self-pardon begins the overall process. You must extend grace to yourself for all of the nurturing and caring you've given to others at heavy expense and to your own detriment.

Taking care of yourself is not selfish. In fact, self care should take priority or you won't remain efficient and beneficial for long. You must weave self-care into your deep yearning to move forward. You must give yourself time to reconcile with yourself after major shifts in life, whether it is a five-minute pause, a brief period of silence, or a sabbatical. Taking sufficient time for yourself allows you to center yourself and encourages the flow of new liberty. It also lets you give yourself permission to recover and define the changes. Giving yourself permission to let go of the old and take hold of new heights should be embraced and celebrated. By creating a space for your creative life to flow freely, it becomes evident that an exchange has taken place in your self-concept, emotions, thoughts, senses, gifts, talents, and calling.

Another aspect of forgiveness is *forth giving*. This act is three-dimensional.

The first dimension involves moving beyond your resistance toward wholeness and exploring the reasons why you may **want to** stay stuck. This is the place where you'll resolve and bring closure to life's disappointments and challenges so you can surge toward wholeness.

The second dimension involves giving up your resentments and your desire to "nurture" old hurts, past experiences and disappointments. It also involves relinquishing your desire for revenge or to exact a penalty for real or imagined—offenses.

The third dimension requires you to give yourself space and time to organize and put into perspective the issues that are in disarray or have changed. These steps allow you to honor a new plan of action: to move beyond what happened before toward your own self-care by choosing to pardon, love, and give beyond the pain and disappointments. These steps give you the opportunity to give yourself the time, honor, and respect you need for transformation.

The greatest love is that of God for creation. God so loves the world that He gave us His only begotten Son. Before anyone asked for forgiveness, God gave, knowing that many would reject, resent, and renounce His Gift. Steadfastly, reconciling the world through His Son, the mission is still being accomplished. *"Herein is love, not that we loved God, but that he loved us, and sent his Son to be the propitiation for our sins"* (1 John 4:10 [KJV]).

So it is that when forgiveness is offered, it provides an opportunity for reconciling with God, others and yourself. Canceling the debt of love that is due you further helps you to embrace wholeness by keeping the law of owing no one anything but love. *"Owe no man anything, but to love one another: for he that loveth another hath fulfilled the law"* (Rom. 13:8 [KJV]). Forgiveness cancels the debt.

Practicing the confession and release of the debt of love is important. You can simply take a piece of paper and write on the top 'Debt Paid in Full by Jesus Christ.' Start by writing down the names, situations and events that need to be remitted then pray for each person and item on your list, rendering all concerns and care regarding the situations to God. More importantly, give space to God to bring forth the fruits of your labor. This type of self-care gives you the liberty to move into new heights and dimensions, to take the initiative to move away from past and present situations into a new, fresh place.

Go beyond circumstance by adopting a new perspective on your present situations. Explore ways to discover new insights and learn from the overall experience. This new discipline will enable you to experience afresh the newness of your daily life. It provides an opportunity for an anointing of fresh oil of the Holy Spirit into new wine skins. It also makes way for God's transformative power to come forth.

Forgiveness is a channel God has made for the flow of fresh water. The scriptures state: ". . . *out of your belly shall flow rivers of living waters*" (John 7:38 [KJV]). Rivers of life, rivers of fresh ideas and rivers of fresh creative energy spring from the belly to refresh the heart, mind, and soul, bringing greater reasons and passion to love and give again. This depth of self-care stimulates you to the core with a new surge of the Holy Spirit and creates a divine release of laughter, joy, and peace. This invigorating state of being is nurtured by the Holy Spirit.

Releasing your ability to laugh is healthy. *"A merry heart doeth good like a medicine: but a broken spirit drieth the bones"* (Prov. 17:22 [KJV]). A merry heart releases *endorphins*, peptides which are secreted in the brain and possess a pain-relieving effect similar to morphine (*New World Dictionary*). Produced by the pituitary gland and the hypothalamus in the vertebrae, it produces analgesia and a sense of wellbeing. Laughter releases joy. Forgiveness allows you to return to a delightful state of happiness and great pleasure. This state of happiness is an inward feeling of contentment and joy. *"Then he said unto them, Go your way, eat the fat, and drink the sweet, and send portions unto them for whom nothing is prepared: for this day is holy unto our LORD: neither be ye sorry; for the joy of the LORD is your strength"* (Neh. 8:10 [KJV]).

And administering forgiveness lets the peace of God rule in your heart. *"And let the peace of God rule in your hearts, to the which also ye are called in one body; and be ye thankful"* (Col. 3:15 [KJV]). *"And the very God of peace sanctify you wholly; and I pray God your whole spirit and soul and body be preserved blameless unto the coming of our Lord Jesus Christ"* (1 Thess. 5:23 [KJV]). Forgiveness as a component of self-care is like putting a new garment on your newly-showered body: spirit, mind, and soul are refreshed in the act.

The act of letting go is another action you can take toward self-care. It is essential to self-care to release and to let go. You can't receive anything when you're full—full of caring and attending to others, full of unsettled concerns, emotions, or thoughts. Your ability to let go allows you to move to a place of wholeness. It creates the space you need to receive more. It is impossible to pour more into a full cup. By letting go of past experiences you create room for something new to emerge. *"Behold, the former things are come to pass, and new things do I declare: before they spring forth I tell you of them"* (Isa. 42:9 [KJV]).

James Emerson writes in *Forgiveness: Key to the Creative Life* " . . . forgiveness is a powerful tool for coming to terms with life. Forgiveness, properly understood and properly used, leads to healing and wholeness in the lives of individuals and of communities." (xiii)

In his book *Forgiveness: The Greatest Healer of All*, Gerald Jampolsky lists 25 stepping stones to forgiveness: one of these is " . . . forgiveness is the key to happiness" (109). When you are in a state of happiness, you can influence your environment positively. Your authenticity compels spiritual depth and liberation. Jampolsky also asserts, "the power of love and forgiveness in our lives can produce miracles." (110)

The miraculous power of God flows through His principles. As the scriptures state, *God has not given us the spirit of fear, but love, power and a sound mind.* Sometimes, fear of the unknown chokes out our faith in our ability to act on godly principles. The more you offer forgiveness, the more it will eliminate the "what if's" in your life, all of the uncertainties that you've tucked away. Forgiveness will keep your mind sound and agape love flowing. This is the fruit God wants you to bear.

Another area to be aware of as natural caregivers, you nurture three families: your family of origin, your creative family, and your church family. Caring for family members while attending to the needs of your creative family can take a lot out of you—be sure to take time to nurture yourself. Remember, it only takes a minute to give yourself permission to pause, to pray, or to a schedule a weekend for rest and relaxation, and **you are worth it**. God took time off on the seventh day. When is the last time you took an entire day off to care for yourself?

Welcome this invitation to honor yourself . . . In her book, *105 Days of Prayer: Prayer for Emotional Space,* Jackie McCullough writes:

> Situations and people can torment me so that I need a hiding place. It is so hard at times to find seclusion or downtime, in order to recoup from the blows, disappointments, and disillusionments I encounter periodically. This place is a place of refuge, a place of healing, and a place of quiet rest. This is what I need every now and then.
>
> Help me to know when I must distance myself in order to experience myself in Your divine presence. You love me, You care for me, and You will sustain me. Your arms are strong enough to bear me up in my feeble times; therefore, I cherish the moments that I can be tenderly nurtured and refreshed by You.
>
> There are some friends, family members, and associates who create a toxic atmosphere that seeks to poison my whole existence. I crave for Your presence when the air becomes polluted with hate, anger, envy, jealousy, and unkindness. Show me the escape routes so that I can hide under the shadow of Your wings and be safe. You are my security, O Lord! (85).

To produce good fruit, caring for yourself takes strategic planning and intentionality. When you take adequate care of yourself, the fruit of longevity and wholeness remain far longer to influence your family, your community, and generations to come. Bell hooks states, "My mother had completely internalized the notion that her value is completely tied to her capacity to serve others" (89).

My own mother suffered a massive heart attack and died at the age of 52 years old. I remember that day vividly. It was the 12th of January, 1988. I was with her that afternoon for lunch, and she told me, "I do not feel good. I should have seen the doctor this morning when I took Mama in to see him."

Had she seen the doctor on that day she would have had an opportunity to have *her* needs met. But she over-valued serving others and, as a result, neglected her own well-being.

Later that evening, I was on my knees praying at church during our special prayer service when someone tapped me on the shoulder and told me I had a phone call. As I ran down the stairs to take the call, the question that badgered me was "Who could possibly be calling?"

As I picked up the phone to say "hello," my younger brother said, "Helen, Mother is gone . . . she has died." In an instant, I felt as though someone had hit me in the head with a hammer. The crushing blow sent me onto the cold concrete floor in the church's kitchen.

The abrupt ending of the life of our matriarch was traumatic. Twenty years later, the family still feels the effects of her early demise. I now sound the alarm to those of you who neglect taking care of yourself. It is vital to incorporate caring for yourself into your ministry if you want to continue to be effective and robust.

It is God's desire to teach you and to have an intimate relationship with you. He met with Adam and Eve in the cool of the day in the garden. He still wants to meet daily with you. He created you in His image so that you can commune with Him. Talking with God is one of the many daily provisions available to you. It is during this time when God shares the plans He has for your life. And you get to share your supplications and petitions with Him. This is His plan so that you will come boldly to His throne and share your heart and mind. *"Let us therefore come boldly unto the throne of grace that we may obtain mercy, and find grace to help in time of need"* Hebrews 4:6.

Your heart is a vital organ. Physically, it pumps your blood and cleans your system of toxic sludge. Spiritually, it is the seat of your soul. So maintaining a clean heart is necessary for a healthy spiritual life. It is **necessary** to stay in good relationship with God and others. Prayer provides a way for cleaning out the unprofitable fruit in your life. Prayer is a tool to confess your disappointments, rejections, hurts, issues and life's baggage. And confession during prayer opens you to examine your own heart to see whether you're in the faith and to prove yourself. *"Examine yourselves, whether ye be in the faith; prove your own selves. Know ye not your own selves, how that Jesus Christ is in you, except ye be reprobates?"* 2 Corinthians 13:5.

Learning more about yourself empowers you to understand your strengths, weaknesses, likes and dislikes. You'll also uncover why you do things the way you do and why you react to things in the way you do. Becoming aware of yourself gives you knowledge to take better care of yourself. It's not being selfish, it's fulfilling a command . . . **love your neighbor as you love yourself.** "*Thou shalt love thy neighbour as thyself. There is none other commandment greater than these.*" Mark 12:31. If you don't love and appreciate yourself it difficult to love and appreciate others. So take whatever time is necessary to discover yourself, to uncover the real you.

What You'll Discover about Yourself

You are a fabulous woman created in the image of God. Embrace yourself; let the creative power of the Holy Spirit flow through you. No other woman can accomplish what you were uniquely created to do. You're here to execute God's will filled with the love and joy of the Lord . . . not bitter, but better. It is completely up to you to maintain a healthy self-image as you labor in the kingdom inspite of every battle, setback, set up or crossing of your own personal Jordan. Always remember, just as you engage in daily hygiene, it is vital to closely examine the areas of your life that need letting go or your forgiveness. I like to say that when used together, prayer and forgiveness gets rid of your spiritual spots and wrinkles.

The flight attendant instructs the passengers on the importance of caring for self. As an aircraft is preparing to take off, we passengers are told, "In the event of an emergency oxygen masks will drop from the overhead compartments. Place an oxygen mask on yourself before attending to others." When it comes to dealing with the unnecessary baggage you have to take the mask off.

I was introduced to the Sankofa symbol several years ago in the course of my graduate studies via a student from Africa. Its message resonated deeply within me. Since then, I've used the information in several speaking engagements and teaching opportunities. The Sankofa method of reflection provides wisdom and knowledge. The quest to critically examine yourself and further investigate knowledge of the past empowers you in your quest to become a better person. And the knowledge you gain by returning to and working through disappointments and obstacles will ground you, strengthening your self-concept. It brings resolution and closure while promoting your desire to engage in self-care. The experience is transforming, and liberating. What a wealth of wisdom! The principle of forgiveness and prayer are profound necessities in the process of caring for yourself.

These practices deliver you to a fresh, clean place. Give yourself permission to pray and forgive daily; doing so will enable you to abide in a fresh place. Remember: give forgiveness first, evaluate the situation or offense later.

We know how to pray and enter the presence of God, but the act of letting go is vital. In fact, it is a commandment. It needs to be a part of our daily devotions.

Forgiveness—letting go— is not based on emotions. Emotions are erratic. How often have you have said, "I don't feel like doing it" or "It's not in my heart" or "I can't find a place in my heart to do it." God, in His infinite wisdom, knew that at times it would be challenging to let go so He commanded Peter to forgive seventy times seven. Matthew 18:21-22 (King James Version) *Then came Peter to him, and said, Lord, how oft shall my brother sin against me, and I forgive him? Till seven times? Jesus saith unto him, I say not unto thee, Until seven times: but, until seventy times seven.* God's grace is made perfect in our weakness and will enable you to apply these principles to the infirmities of life even when it feels uncomfortable. *"And he said unto me, My grace is sufficient for thee: for my strength is made perfect in weakness. Most gladly therefore will I rather glory in my infirmities, that the power of Christ may rest upon me."* 2 Corinthians 12:9.

Keep forgiveness (letting go) local and immediate. Doing so lets you move swiftly into a new place to regain a godly perceptive. As importantly, immediate forgiveness is for *your* benefit. 2 Corinthians 2:10-12 (King James Version) *To whom ye forgive anything, I forgive also: for if I forgave anything, to whom I forgave it, for your sakes forgave I it in the person of Christ; Lest Satan should get an advantage of us: for we are not ignorant of his devices. Furthermore, when I came to Troas to preach Christ's gospel, and a door was opened unto me of the Lord.*

In addition, re-evaluating the situation in a healthy place with a fresh lens and a clear mind enables you to keep the blessing. Your heart is able to contain the seed so it can take root and bear fruit. Matthew 13:22-23 (King James Version) *He also that received seed among the thorns is he that heareth the word; and the care of this world, and the deceitfulness of riches, choke the word, and he becometh unfruitful. But he that received seed into the good ground is he that heareth the word, and understandeth it; which also beareth fruit, and bringeth forth, some an hundredfold, some sixty, some thirty.*

During the process of re-evaluation, you will release that which is not beneficial. You will have new lens to identify the fruit that was gained from the overall experience. Ask yourself, did you obtain the fruit of longsuffering, or temperance, gentleness, kindness, faithfulness and trustworthiness . . . ? (See Galatians 5:22-23).

Another process is redefining you. This is a process of acknowledging God's work in your life. It is just as important as receiving and giving forgiveness. During this process, give attention to naming the newness and claiming the new place and everything else that God has done in your life. This should be done daily by acknowledging the new blessings, strength or liberty. Speak affirmations and read the Scriptures daily. Write or journal daily.

When you engage in declaring or hearing the blessing, it becomes an act of making known and formally showing what God has done. (See **I Am Who I Am** and the **Daughters of Destiny Affirmations**). More importantly, as you affirm yourself verbally in the Word of God, the more evidence you'll recognize with regard to the actualization and the manifestation of God's Word. The Word cannot return void; it must accomplish what it was sent to do. To the degree that you claim and declare your promises, they will manifest. The Scripture states, it is nigh thee even in your mouth. Romans 10:8 *But what saith it? The word is nigh thee, even in thy mouth, and in thy heart: that is, the word of faith . . .* I say it like this: "There is a miracle in your mouth . . . speak it, decree it, believe it and release it!"

Not everyone will be able to immediately identify your new liberty or blessing, but God and you will be able to intimately celebrate the depth of freshness or healing and deliverance. So treasure whatever God is doing and stay in the fresh place. Remember, titles are not important to God, but your position in God is vital. It is God that gives promotion and rewards. Psalm 75:5-7 (King James Version) *Lift not up your horn on high: speak not with a stiff neck. For promotion cometh neither from the east, nor from, the west, nor from the south. But God is the judge: he putteth down one, and setteth up another.* Psalm 18:19-21 (King James Version) *He brought me forth also into a large place; he delivered me, because he delighted in me. The LORD rewarded me according to my righteousness; according to the cleanness of my hands hath he recompensed me. For I have kept the ways of the LORD, and have not wickedly departed from my God.* Maintaining your ability to stay in God's presence is more important than reputation or position. True promotions and rewards come from God.

> *"Verily I say unto you, whatsoever ye shall bind on earth shall be bound in heaven: and whatsoever ye shall loose on earth shall be loosed in heaven."* Mt.18:18

Prayer is the key that unlocks doors in heaven and earth. Prayer is the instrument God has given to the church (God's people) to obtain victory over the battles in your life, to bring forth God's promises and release God's purpose for you.

So it is, within this devised plan one can come boldly to His throne to share their heart and mind. *"Let us therefore come boldly unto the throne of grace that we may obtain mercy, and find grace to help in time of need"* Hebrews 4:6.

Definition of the word key: *an instrument, usually of metal, for moving the bolt of a lock and thus locking or unlocking something; a device to turn a bolt, wedge, cotter or similar put into a hole or space to lock or hold parts together.*

When you have the key to something you have ownership. When Christ gave you the key, He expected you to take ownership. Use it! But here's the thing, you must believe in your heart that He gave you the key; you must see it in the spiritual realm (by faith) in order for it to work. It is your prayer and your faith that makes the key unlock the door to the blessings and promises that God has foreordained for you.

Definition of the word bolt: is a sliding bar for locking a door, gate, etc.; a similar bar in a lock moved by a key.

Spiritual bolts lock you away from your blessings. These bolts can include, wavering, unbelief, un-forgiveness; un-confessed sin; gossip, jealousy; envy, strife, unresolved offensives and bitterness.

Let's take a look at the dead bolt in the scriptures. *"If any of you lack wisdom, let him ask of God that giveth to all men liberally, and upbraideth not: and it shall be given him. But let him ask in faith, nothing wavering. For he that wavereth is like a wave of the sea driven with the wind and tossed. For let not that man think that he shall receive any thing of the Lord. A double minded man is unstable in all his ways."* James 1:5-7.

James was addressing the Jewish converts who lived outside the Holy land. His main theme was practical religion manifesting itself in good work contrasted with the mere profession of faith. James offers much insight and tools for being victorious. In one passage he points out an area of importance for the believers: **how to use your key!** "**But let him ask in faith nothing wavering . . . " James 1:6.**

It is counter-cultural to ask in faith when the world's systems are set up to dictate how to live your life and obtain your livelihood. To step out of the natural realm into the spiritual realm and believe God is completely against your natural cognitive realm, but in the supernatural realm doors of opportunities await.

> " *I am crucified with Christ: nevertheless I live; yet not I, but Christ liveth in me: and the life which I now live in the flesh I live by the faith of the Son of God, who loved me, and gave himself for me.*" Galatians 2:20

> "*But that no man is justified by the law in the sight of God, it is evident: for, the just shall live by faith.*" Galatians 3:11

To live by faith requires you to speak what you believe and not what you see.

> "*I believed, therefore have I spoken . . .*" Psalm 116:10

> "*We having the same spirit of faith, according as it is written, I believed and therefore have I spoken, we also believe, and therefore speak;* II Cor. 4:13.

Unlocking the Dead Bolt of Wavering to get to My Spiritual Blessings

How do I know if I'm wavering?

Waver means to swing or sway to and fro; to show doubt or indecision; find it hard, or be unable to decide.

We've all found ourselves wavering at one time or another. For example, when you're blessed with extra cash you may be unable to decide which dress or shoes to purchase, what restaurant to eat at, or what piece of furniture to get. James admonishes the believer to understand how important it is to clearly understand what it is you really want.

If your present ability to verbalize your wants are suppressed because of your environment (past or present) or because you were or are penalized or disciplined for asking for something you want, it may be difficult to verbalize your desire.

For example, if you've come from a family of strict disciplinarians who made you sit at the table until you'd eaten all of the food on your plate you may have developed an eating disorder or some other unwanted baggage.

Take a moment to forgive those who trespassed against your desire to speak and act for yourself.

Unlocking the Spiritual Bolt of Wavering

Dear Jesus,

I forgive _____ for _____ and release them to you. I seek no vengeance against them. I render all my rights to retaliate to you. Wash me and cleanse me now O Lord, take the pain, hurt, and disappointment out of my spirit, mind and soul. Lord, bless _____. Continue to lead and guide them with your love and tender mercies. I thank you for total healing and I'm now free to speak and live my desires.

Prayer of Forgiveness for Wavering

Forgive yourself for wavering!

Lord, forgive me for wavering and being indecisive. I forgive myself and release God's power within me to work on my behalf to speak my earnest desire and be true to myself.

When things resonate in your heart that hinder you from being able to decide and/or ask, ask God to reveal it to you. When He reveals it, remember to pray the prayer of forgiveness for them and yourself. Also, pray the Forgiveness for Wavering Prayer.

Now expect God to move on your behalf. Since you have forgiven, now forgiveness is coming to you. Remember a key biblical principle: give and it shall be given unto you.

> *"Give, and it shall be given unto you; good measure, pressed down, and shaken together, and running over, shall men give into your bosom. For with the same measure that ye mete withal it shall be measured to you again."* Luke 6:38

What do you want?

Tell yourself it is okay to have God's best for you and your family. God has made you worthy to receive His best. It will be a testimony of His goodness and mercy. Why not you! You're His Daughter/Son.

Begin to think about what you desire God to do for you. Remember how to use your key and ask God for wisdom; then, expect God to give you the wisdom you need.

Now employ the promise: "Be careful for nothing but in everything by prayer and supplication make your request known unto God":

My request: (I want)

1.

2.

3.

4.

5.

Use it by Faith.

You must adhere to the conditions set forth in the scriptures for your prayer to be answered. This means you cannot look at your circumstances, your financial condition, or your health; you must look through the eyes of your faith to see the end results.

When you finish asking, be sure to close and lock your door ~ by praying "This I ask according to your will in Jesus' Name."

Unlocking Unbelief:
A Dead Bolt to Spiritual Blessing

Unbelief is withholding, or lack of, belief especially in religion or certain religious doctrines. Unbelief implies merely a lack of belief due to insufficient evidence.

Disbelief: An active refusal to believe.

Are you waiting to see the evidence of your prayers? The Bible clearly states that you must believe to see.

The reason for unbelief is insufficient evidence. Let's take a look at one of the twelve disciples, Thomas.

> *"But Thomas, one of the twelve, called Didymus, was not with them when Jesus came. The other disciples therefore said unto him, we have seen the Lord. But he said unto them, except I shall see in his hands the print of the nails, and put my finger into the print of the nails, and thrush my hand into his side, I will not believe. Then said he to Thomas, Reach hither thy finger, and behold my hands; and reach hither thy hand, and thrust it into my side; and be not faithless, but believing. And Thomas answered and said unto him, My Lord and my God. Jesus saith unto him, Thomas, because thou hast seen thou hast believed; blessed are they that have not seen, and yet have believed . . . But these are written, that ye might believe that Jesus is the Christ, the Son of God; and that believing ye might have life through his name"* St. John 20:24-31

Another example of unbelief is when the children of Israel were excluded because of unbelief:

> While it is said, today if ye will hear his voices, harden not your hearts, as in the provocation. For some, when they had heard, did provoke; howbeit not all that came out of Egypt by Moses. But with whom was he grieved forty years? Was it not with them that had sinned whose carcasses fell in the wilderness? And to whom sware he that they should not enter into his rest, but to them that believed not? So we see that they could not enter in because of unbelief. Heb. 3:15-18.

Unlocking the Spiritual Bolt of Unbelief and Doubt

Dear Jesus,

I forgive myself for doubting you and not esteeming that you have made me to be worthy to receive your best. Wash me and cleanse me now O Lord. I allow you to build my confidence in trusting you with my whole heart, mind and soul. Thank you for total healing of my belief in you and your Word. I now live my life in the realm of faith.

Unfeigned faith in God and His Word is the key to overcoming the dead bolt of unbelief.

The Faithful and Faith:
Speaking the Faith of the Faithful

Many times we do not have the faith of the heroes of our faith. But we can certainly speak their words to create the same results.

> *"Now Abraham and Sarah were old and well stricken in age; and it ceased to be with Sarah after the manner of women. Therefore Sarah laughed within herself saying, After I am waxed old shall I have pleasure, my lord being old also? And the Lord said unto Abraham, Wherefore did Sarah laugh, saying, Shall I of a surety bear a child, which am old? Is anything too, hard for the Lord? At the time appointed I will return unto thee, according to the time of life, and Sarah shall have a son."* Gen. 18:11-14

> *Through faith also Sara herself received strength to conceive seed, and was delivered of a child when she was past age, because she judged him faithful who had promised."* Heb. 11:11

Sarah's judgment of God was that of being faithful. Sarah laughed within herself, because she was old, but at the appointed time she had Isaac. We too can stand in the judgment of Sarah and openly confess our faith by using her judgment. Her judgment was "God is faithful." and "God, I judge you Faithful."

Sarah's life is a testimony to her faith in God. Her faith has already been tried, tested and proved. So you can overcome by the word of her testimony and by the blood of the Lamb. Simply continue to confess faith; confess that you judge God faithful. He will begin to manifest His faithfulness to you. Pray the prayer of faith and daily confess your judgment of God to Him.

So it was, when Nehemiah was commissioned to build the wall of Jerusalem, he was despised by Sanballat and Tobiah.

When Sanballat the Horonite, and Tobiah the servant, the Ammonite, heard of it, it grieved them exceedingly that there was came a man to seek the welfare of Israel.

The enemy of your soul grieves because you're blessed by God to serve in God's kingdom. Be not removed; the battle has already been won for you by Jesus! Believe it and receive it. Continue on steadfast and unmovable; abound in the work of the Lord.

Nehemiah secretly went to survey the condition of the land.
He acknowledged the condition of Jerusalem.

God will call us to acknowledge our condition and outlook on life. He will call us aside or isolate us from people so we can take a closer look at our lives and allow Him to show us areas to focus on to remove the reproach.

Hear the words of Nehemiah to the people after his assessment.

> "... Ye see the distress that we are in, how Jerusalem lieth waste and the gates therefore are burned with fire ... " Nehemiah 2:17a

Be honest. Acknowledge your condition and/or circumstances; they are no secret to God. Then take action to correct what is amiss or seek wisdom as to how to be victorious in the areas of your life that thwart you.

Then Nehemiah released his faith by speaking and inviting the people to act.

> "Come, and let us build up the wall of Jerusalem, that we be no more a reproach." Nehemiah 2:17b

Nehemiah assured the people that God's commissioning of him to do the work, affirming that God was indeed with him. He stated, "The hand of my God which was good upon me: as also the king's words that he had spoken unto him."

When the people heard the faith and courage of Nehemiah, they began to release their own faith.

> *"And they said, Let us rise up and build. So they strengthened their hands for this good work." (Neh. 2:18)*

Your faith is contagious. When you speak it, others will hear your faith and begin to act upon their own. So the more you practice speaking your faith, the more your faith will grow. You will see a manifestation of the things you are believing God to do. Keep releasing words of faith. Unfeigned faith is pure faith in God and His ability to work on your behalf and through you.

Then Nehemiah put the responsibly on God to provide the necessary means to get the job done:

> *He confessed his faith*

> *"Then answered I them, and said unto them, The God of heaven, he will prosper us; therefore we his servants will arise and build . . . " (Neh. 2:20).*

> *"Now, my son, the Lord be with thee, and prosper thou . . . " I Chr. 22:11*

A Confession of my faith
Repeat:

The God of heaven, He will prosper me; therefore I will arise and build.

> *"Now Faith is the substance of things hoped for the evidence of things not seen."* Heb. 11:1

Through faith we understand . . .
Unfeigned Faith—must be genuine, real and sincere. You must genuinely desire God to move on your behalf. You must be authentic (true, not faking) before God—renouncing the hidden things of dishonesty, not walking in craftiness, nor handling the word of God deceitfully . . . II Cor. 4:2.

Acts 27:25

Acts 16:34

Luke 1:38

Rom. 15:29

II Corn. 5:7

Gal. 5:5

Luke 7:50
> *"And he said to the woman, Thy faith hath saved thee; go in peace."*

Luke 1:38
"And Mary said, Behold the handmaid of the Lord; be it unto me according to thy word."

Acts 27:25
"I believe God, that it shall be even as it was told me."

2 Cor. 5:7
(We walk by faith, not by sight).

Matt. 15:28
"Then Jesus answered and said unto her, O woman, great is thy faith; be it unto thee even as thou wilt."

II Cor. 4:13
"We having the same spirit of faith, according as it is written, I believed, and therefore have I spoken, we also believe, and therefore speak."

Paul is sharing his premises that he is not preaching himself, but Christ Jesus the Lord. He stated he was their servant for Jesus' sake. Paul clearly knew who he was and whom he believed as well as what he was called to do. When you believe God and understand who you are in Christ and your purpose—you'll speak.

The Samaritan woman had an encounter with God at the well. He needed to go through Samaria for this woman.

> *"And he must needs go through Samaria. . . . There cometh a woman of Samaria to draw water; Jesus saith unto her, give me to drink . . . The woman saith unto him I know that Messias cometh, which is called the Christ; when he is come, he will tell us all things. Jesus saith unto her, I that speak unto thee am he . . . The woman then left her waterpot, and went her way into the city, and saith to the men. Come, see a man, which told me all things that ever I did; is not this the Christ? The woman at the well left her water pot because she had an encounter with Jesus."* John 4:4-29

God came to your city one day and you had an encounter at your personal well. Now you need to leave your pot (your pain, your disappointment, and shame),—whatever you're clutching and clinging to from the past—and forgive yourself and go on. Call someone and tell them you are going on, going to a place beyond where you are now, by leaving your past behind. Your next destination may be writing a book, going to the doctor for a checkup, resolving in your heart to forgive and to love again, forgiving your parents, trusting again; starting that business; loving yourself. Leave your doubts and past experiences behind because what you have now is NOW FAITH, not yesterday's faith! Yesterday is over! It ended at 12:01a.m. It is under the Blood and in the sea of forgetfulness; cross over, my Sister, cross over, my Brother, into your Jordan. You got to believe God!

> *"But without faith it is impossible to please him; for he that cometh to God must believe that he is and that he is a rewarder of them that diligently seek him." Heb. 11:6*

Confession of Faith

Confession is important to the believer. As you openly declare what you believe, faith and confession produce the evidence of your belief.

As you are waiting on God to manifest the answer to your prayer, daily confess your faith. You don't have to beg, just believe. Speak your faith while you wait.

A confession of the Faithful

Repeat after me:
Lord, I judge you faithful

A confession of my faith
Repeat after me:

Lord, I judge you faithful; You can do all things; nothing is impossible with you. I believe you can and will do it!!

**Repeat throughout the day:
Lord, have your way!

- *I Believe God.*

A confession of my faith

Repeat after me:
Lord, I believe God even as You have spoken.

- *Be it unto me according to thy word.*
"And Mary said, Behold the handmaid of the Lord; be it unto me according to thy word" (Luke 1:38).

A confession of my faith

Repeat after me:
Lord, be it unto me according to thy word.

- *Lord, have your way.*
Jesus said unto him, I am the way, the truth and the life . . . *(John 14:6)*

A confession of my faith

Repeat after me:
Lord, have your way.

- *By your stripes I'm healed.*
" . . . and with his stripes we are healed" *(Is. 53:5).*

A confession of my faith

Repeat after me:
Lord, by your stripes I'm healed.

- *I've been redeem by the blood of the Lamb.*
" . . . hast redeemed us to God by thy blood" *(Rev. 5:11).*

A confession of my faith

Repeat after me:
I've been redeem by the blood of the Lamb.

- *Lord, Lead me, and Guide me.*
"Howbeit when he come, he will guide you into all truth . . ." *(John 16:13).*

"Lead me in thy truth and teach me . . ." *(Ps.25:5).*

A confession of my faith

Repeat after me:
Lord, lead me, and guide me.

- *I can do it*
  "I can do all things through Christ which strengthened me." *(Ph. 4:13).*

A confession of my faith

Repeat after me:
I can do it. I can do all things through Christ which Strengthens me.

- *I'm sure God will move on my behalf*

A confession of my faith

Repeat after me:
Thank you Lord for moving on my behalf

- *I am more than a conqueror*
  "Nay, in all these things we are more than conquerors through him that loved us" *(Ro. 8:37).*

A confession of my faith

Repeat after me:
I am more than a conqueror

- *Greater is he that is within me than he that is in the world*
  I John 4:4
  "Ye are of God, little children, and have overcome them: because greater is he that is in you, than he that is in the world."

A confession of my faith

Repeat after me:
Greater is he that is within me than he that is in the world.

- *Jesus will fix it.*

A confession of my faith

Repeat after me:
Jesus will fix it.

- *I believe God.*

A confession of my faith

Repeat after me:
I believe God.

- *God will prosper me*

A confession of my faith

Repeat after me:
God will prosper me.

He. 10:23
Let us hold fast that profession of our faith without wavering: for he is faithful that promised.

A confession of my faith

Repeat after me:
Lord, You promised and I know that you are faithful to your promises. I Thank you for bringing it to pass.

II Th. 3:3
"But the Lord is faithful, who shall establish you, and keep you from evil."

A confession of my faith

Repeat after me:
Lord, Thank you for keeping me from evil and establishing me.

De 7:9

"Know therefore that the Lord thy God, he is God, the faithful God, which keepeth covenant and mercy with them that love him and keep his commandments to a thousand generations."

A confession of my faith

Repeat after me:

Lord, You are God, the Faithful God. You will keep your covenant and mercy to them that love you. Lord, I love you.

New Words in My Mouth
Words of Faith

A list of New Word of Faith

Because the power of life and death is in the tongue it is crucial to speak life as you wait for God to bring your prayer request to pass. Listed below are *Faith Phrases* to use until the evidence is manifested. Throughout the day, speak Faith Phrases aloud. They will serve as the substance of the things hoped for.

- *God will direct me*
- *God will show me*
- *God will provide for me*
- *God will protect me*
- *God will help me*
- *God is my source and resource*
- *God is my strength*
- *God is my deliverer*
- *God is my Lord*
- *God is my King*
- *God is my Creator and knows what best for me*
- *I rest in the plan of God for my life*
- *God is in control*
- *God is my rock and defense*
- *God is my fortress*
- *God is my shield*
- *God will sustain us*
- *Jesus is the way*
- *Jesus is my way out of no way*

- *Jesus is the light of the world*
- *I'm of good courage*
- *I'm strong in the Lord and the power of His might*
- *He is going to do it, I believe He will*
- *He can, He will, and He shall come through for me*
- *I can do it! I will do it! God said so!*
- *God is on my side*

Scripture Regarding Praying by Faith

"And all things, whatsoever ye shall ask in prayer, believing, ye shall receive." Matthew 21:22

"And whatsoever ye shall ask in my name, that will I do, that the Father may be glorified in the Son. If ye shall ask any thing in my name, I will do it." John 12:13, 14

"Ye have not chosen me, but I have chosen you, and ordained you, that ye should go and bring forth fruit and that your fruit should remain; that whatsoever, ye shall ask of the Father in my name, he may give it you." John 15:16

"And in that day ye shall ask me nothing, verily, verily, I say unto you, whatsoever ye shall ask the Father in my name, he will give it you. Hitherto have ye asked nothing in my name; ask, and ye shall receive, that your joy may be full. These thing have I spoken unto you in proverbs; but the time cometh, when I shall no more speak unto you in proverbs, but I shall shew you plainly of the Father. As that day ye shall ask in my name; and I say not unto you, that I will pray the Father for you; For the Father himself loveth you, because ye have loved me, and have believed that I came out from God." John 16:23-27

God's spoken Word has enough creative power to demand activity from a vacuum. The void produced a universe.

Even nothingness cannot resist the power of God's creative Word.

He spoke into the emptiness, *"Let there be,"* and it was so.

Every project produced by human beings starts with a list of materials before the work beings. However, God began His work with only a plan and no raw materials. He knows the end of His work before He begins, and no one can overrule Him (Isaiah 46:10). The Word of God is so powerful and creative that He only needs to speak it once, and the Word continues to produce results without any additional attention.

Thus, all of creation continues at the same speed and orbit as from the beginning. He is . . . upholding and maintaining and guiding and propelling the universe by His mighty word of power" (Hebrews 1:3, The Amplified Version).

Prayers of Forgiveness
by Helen Orme

GENERAL

Dear God,

It is not easy for me to forgive. I know that Your word commands us to forgive. Please help me obey Your word, even when I do not want to let it go. Lord, not my will but Your will be done, this I ask in Jesus' Name. Let Your grace and mercy fill my heart with forgiveness. Lord, help me now. I pray, in Jesus' Name. Amen.

Dear Lord Jesus,

I repent of all of my transgressions, iniquities, sins, trespasses and I turn from my wicked ways and return to You.

Dear God,

I forgive myself for over-functioning and working beyond my limits. I now give myself permission to honor myself by engaging in daily intentional self-care. In Jesus' Name. Amen.

Dear God,

I ask that you forgive me for not loving my body and esteeming my well-being. I ask that you grant unto me a greater appreciation of self. In Jesus' Name. Amen.

Dear God,

I forgive myself for all of the bad choices I've made in allowing others and myself to violate my dreams, goals, aspirations, and purpose. I now forgive them and myself. I forge forward into my destiny. In Jesus' Name. Amen.

Dear God,

Forgive me for not having an excellence spirit. Thank You Lord for creating within me a right spirit.

Dear God,

Forgive me for not paying my tithes and giving an offering that there may be meat in Your house. I've robbed You and Your House. I repent and turn from my wicked ways. Help me O Lord, to change my behavior toward the things You command in Your word. This I pray in Jesus' Name. Amen.

Dear God,

I confess, I've allowed the expectations, disapproval, and rejections of others to define who I am. I now step out of the arena of failure into the arena of success. I am who You say I am. In Jesus' Name. Amen.

Dear God,

Forgive me for not being a good steward over the resources You've given me. Help me to be a wise steward of my time, resources, energy, people, gifts and talents. Show me how to be an excellent steward.

Dear God,

I forgive my neighbor for stealing my property. They've moved the line of our land over, taking several feet of our property. You are an all-knowing God. Lord, thank You for fighting my battle. I give this to You and help me to love them unconditionally. This I pray in Jesus' Name.

MINISTRY

Dear God,

I forgive those who tried earnestly to murder my fervor; those who shoot their arrows at me when I soar on Your winds; those who set snares and traps on my journey. I forgive those who threw me in the lion's den; those who fell asleep in the garden; those who betrayed me with a kiss; those who stole my ideas when I innocently shared my dreams. I forgive those who stabbed me in the back and turned the knife; those who sent me into war on the frontlines to kill my passion so that they could take what belonged to me; those who hated seeing me bounce back or show up when their plans failed. I forgive those who tried to leave me in a ditch, only to see a good Samaritan from a faraway place bind up my wounds and provide a place of lodging until I could recover. I thank You, and humbly forgive them. In Jesus' Name. Amen.

Dear God,

I confess that I've allowed racism, sexism, and classism to hinder my progress. I forgive all those who have imposed their limitations on my life and I seek no revenge. I believe the promises of Your Word: I can do all things through Christ who strengthens me, and no weapon formed against me will prosper. I now receive Your strength. In Jesus' Name. Amen.

Dear God,

I forgive those who look at me with disgust in their eyes and with "Who does she thinks she is?" wedged in their minds, for they know not what they do. In Jesus' Name. Amen.

Dear God,

I forgive those who innocently wage war against my pure intention to answer the call and to love my God with all my heart, all my mind, and all my soul. In Jesus' Name. Amen.

Dear God,

I forgive those who misinterpret my love for You and my passion to do Your will. They try to murder my reputation and place roadblocks at the doorways of my destiny. I forgive them. In Jesus' Name. Amen.

Dear God,

I forgive those who intentionally trespass against my calling, my purpose and my destiny. I seek no revenge but to love those that spitefully use me and speak all manner of evil against me behind closed doors, in private meetings; who create laws, policies and guidelines to contain and divert my potential, my future, and my wellbeing. I pray for Your tender mercies and Your loving kindness toward them. In Jesus' Name. Amen.

Dear God,

I forgive those who are stuck in tradition and unable to appreciate God's call for women to lead; who do not understand that I am called, capable, and confident I will get the job done. In Jesus' Name. Amen.

Dear God,

I confess I haven't totally embraced my worth, but have hidden behind servitude, allowing others to walk on my ideas, dreams, and destiny. I no longer wait for the affirmation or approval of others: I forgive them and myself. I will forge forward to live out the thoughts You have for me, to do good and to give me an expected end. In Jesus' Name. Amen.

Dear God,

I forgive myself for quieting my voice and gift for the sake of others. I release my tongue, voice, and life to reveal your glory. In Jesus' Name. Amen.

Dear God,

Forgive me for not walking through the door You've opened. I was afraid and allowed fear to grip my heart. I ask that You would redeem the opportunity and let me recognize it. Give me the grace to step through it and possess my promise. This I ask in Jesus' Name. Amen.

Dear God,

Forgive me for not preparing myself for the ministry/service. Give me the grace to redeem the time and help me to make a three day journey in one day. I receive Your pardon and Your grace. Thank You for opening new doors to flow in my gifts to edify the Body of Christ.

Dear God,

Forgive give me for being hard on myself and blaming others for me not going forth. I now walk away from my old behavior and habits. I give myself permission to be the person You've ordained before the foundation of this world. I step out of the arena of failure into the arena of success. Thank You Lord, in Jesus' Name. Amen.

Dear God,

I've given my all and sometimes, my all does not seems enough. One day they are saying, Hosanna, Hosanna, and now they are saying, crucify, crucify. I forgive them. Bear me up on Your wings and take me to a place that is higher than myself.

Dear God,

Forgive me for allowing fear to grip my heart when You've told me and shown me that You are with me always. Put strength in my voice, courage in my heart, and boldness in my mind to accomplish this task. When it looks like a giant, help me to see it as a grasshopper. Thank You, Lord.

Dear God,

Forgive me for not bringing my body under subjection. Help me not to think too highly of myself because You love the humble heart of Your children. Bring me in when I get too far out and beyond Your guidance. Thank You, Lord.

Dear God,

I ask for the forgiveness of those I've may have hurt or disappointed or let down. You are my righteous Judge. Help me in my blind spots, decisions, and fair judgment. Thank You, Lord. This I ask in Jesus' Name. Amen.

Dear God,

I ask for forgiveness for not executing the assignment You have for me. I receive Your pardon and release of this matter. I'm now walking in Your liberty. This I ask in Jesus' Name. Amen.

Dear God,

I ask You to forgive me for carrying the guilt of others for their lack of being responsible. Enable me to give myself permission to do my God-given assignments and the ability to delegate. This I ask in Jesus' Name. Amen.

FAMILY

Dear God,

I release my family and those I care for into Your capable hands. In Jesus' Name. Amen.

Dear God,

I forgive them for laying me off for no reason. Help me to provide for my family and be the person You've called me to be and not be ashamed when circumstances beyond my control affect my family. I've done all I can do;I ask that You would intervene. O Lord, YOU are the God of my salvation.

Dear God,

I forgive myself for feeling the choices of my children are because I've failed as a parent. I release myself from all guilt and shame. I now receive

Your grace to forge forward, be the health of my countenance and restore the joy of my salvation. I give them to You and let their ministering angel minister to them and enable them to make You their Lord and Savior. This I pray in Jesus' Name. Amen.

Dear Lord,

    I forgive my husband for walking out on me and the children. I forgive him of all the pain, disappointment, hardship he caused me. I release me and all revenge, resentment, and grudges against him to you. I forgive myself and receive your pardon and grace to move forward with my life. This I ask in Jesus' Name. Amen.

Dear God,

    I ask that You forgive me for not being the child I should have been to my parent(s). For not honoring, obeying and respecting them as Your chosen guardian for my life. I release all of the guilt and shame I caused them and I now forgive myself and receive Your pardon and grace. Redeem all of the wrong seeds I've sown and let me reap Your mercy. This I humbly ask in Jesus' Name. Amen.

Dear God,

    My child has been falsely accuse of this crime. I forgive the accusers and release all of the resentment, hurt, disappointment this has caused me and my family. I nail it onto the Cross of Calvary in exchange for Your victory. Release unto me Your grace and Your supernatural strength to bear this situation. Protect my child and keep their mind, spirit and body until Your justice prevails. Lead me to a rock that is higher than myself. O Lord, the God of my Salvation. Renew my joy, for Your joy is my strength, for my bones are vexed with grief. O, JESUS HEAR ME NOW WHEN I PRAY!

Dear God,

    I forgive my husband for all of the belittling, insults, anger and resentment he has against me. Please forgive me for holding onto my disappointment and failed expectations. I now release it to You and apply the blood of Jesus to every entry way. I ask that You put words of life into his mouth and mine. That we both recognize we're fearfully and wonderfully made by You. We vowed through sickness and health in the good times and bad. Now Lord, put new honey in our moon.

Dear God,

I forgive my spouse's family for rejecting me and keeping me out of their events. I feel unvalued by them and uncomfortable when I'm around them. Lord, strengthen my inward person so that I'm able to stand even when they use my spouse's weaknesses and set us against each other. I release them from their intentional and unintentional rejection and pain. I now release them into Your hands. This I pray in Jesus' Name. Amen.

Dear God,

I forgive my father for not being there for me. I really don't want to forgive him nor do I care about him because of all of the pain he had caused me. I want to be true and this is how I feel. Help me to have the right spirit to truly forgive him and to love him—even when I don't want to even see him or hear his name being called. Renew within me the right spirit and create in me a clean heart, O Lord.

ABANDONMENT

Dear Lord Jesus,

I forgive my mother for abandoning me and giving me up for adoption. I release to You all of my bitterness and resentment. Heal me of the rejection and pain. I give You my emptiness. Fill all of the vacancies in my life with Your love and peace. Give her peace and grace to forgive herself. I thank You for blessing me with caring people and a loving family. This I ask in Jesus' Name. Amen.

Dear God,

I forgive my family for cutting me off and those who chosen to cut themselves off from the family. I release all of my resentment and anger unto You. Heal our fragmentation and deliver us from generational transgressions, iniquities and sins from all of the ancestors that preceded us, the elders, siblings cousins, nieces, nephews and friends. Lord, remove all of the grudges and misunderstandings that were passed down by behavior, words or deeds. Repair the breach that was meant to destroy us. Let Your Divine intervention prevail in our family. Endow us with Your agape love, for we are joint heirs of Your salvation. I thank You in advance for an immediate flow of love, peace and joy in our family, at all of the events, gathering and pray that our conversations will be of love and edifying to one another. This I pray in Jesus' Name. Amen.

PERSONAL

Dear Lord Jesus,

I give myself permission to forgive and to let go of all of the hurt, pain, grudges, un-forgiveness, disappointment I've cause others and myself. I now receive and accept Your pardon and grace to live my life in peace and to the fullest. Your abundance is coming to me now, in Jesus' Name, Amen.

Dear God,

Forgive me for not cherishing the shape and size of my body, the color of my skin and the texture of my hair. I've allowed other definitions of beauty to devalue my self-concept. I realize I am wonderfully made in Your image and display Your beauty and awesome majesty. In Jesus' Name. Amen.

Dear God,

I confess I've been unsettled by my circumstances. I now resolve in my heart and mind to be content, knowing it will be my gain. In Jesus' Name. Amen.

Dear God,

I forgive myself for holding on too tight and not letting go of things I have no control of, and things that were unhealthy. In Jesus' Name. Amen.

Dear God,

I give myself permission to live my dreams, to live my life to its fullest. In Jesus' Name. Amen.

Dear God,

I confess I haven't totally embraced my worth, but have hidden behind servitude, allowing others to walk on my ideas, dreams, and destiny. I no longer wait for the affirmation or approval of others: I forgive them and myself. I will forge ahead to live out the thoughts You have for me, to do good and to give me an expected end. In Jesus' Name. Amen.

Dear God,

I forgive myself for not engaging in a healthy lifestyle. I will exercise more, eat healthily, and get plenty of rest. I forgive those who trespass against my wellbeing. In Jesus' Name. Amen.

Dear God,

I will teach others to honor one of the greatest gifts You've given, the gift of Life, by honoring and esteeming their Temples—their Bodies. In Jesus' Name. Amen.

Dear God,

Forgive me for constantly making bad choices. Please bring to my mind the behavior, thoughts, people and experiences that are influencing these choices. I repent of them now and ask You to help me to transform my mind, by renewing it daily in Your word. Thank You, Jesus. This I ask in Jesus' Name.

JOB

Dear Lord Jesus,

I forgive my co-workers for all of the grief they've caused me. All of the conspiracy, false accusation (s) and rejection they've done against me. I chose to forgive them according to Your word and to bless them that spitefully use me and those who speak all matter of evil against me. I forgive them for they know not what they've done. I release this situation into Your hands. Be the health of my countenance and let Your glory come upon me as I will walk in Your light. This I pray In Jesus' Name, Amen.

Dear God,

I ask You to forgive me for not getting to work on time and taking a longer break than I should. I repent and turn from my wicked way. I receive Your help to be timely and conscious of my behavior and the effects it has on my co-workers. Thank You, Lord.

Dear God,

I confess, I've allowed racism, sexism, and classism to hinder my progress. I forgive all those who have imposed their limitations on my life and I seek no revenge. I believe the promises of Your Word: I can do all things through Christ who strengthens me, and no weapon formed against me will prosper. I now receive Your strength. In Jesus' Name. Amen.

Dear God,

Forgive me for my procrastination. I'm abusing my body with sleeplessness because of my bad choice. Help me to be a good steward of my time.

Dear God,

Forgive me for not applying for the job and not thinking I'm worthy or capable of leading. Deliver me from myself and my self-discriminating thoughts. I now step away from the past into my destiny. In Jesus' Name. Amen.

Special Prayers of Forgiveness

ABUSED

Dear God,

I forgive those who have violated me with harsh criticism, unfair treatment, and emotional, physical, and verbal abuse. Their tongues were like honey but war was in their hearts. I pray for their wellbeing and for their lives to be transformed. In Jesus' Name. Amen.

Dear God,

I forgive _____ for molesting (raping) me. Heal me from all of the pain that this situation has caused me. Wash me clean with hyssop and make me white as snow with Your blood. I seek no revenge, but I choose to love again. When I feel uncomfortable, I give You permission to comfort me. I give my ministering angels permission to minister to me. Lead and guide me into all truth. Deliver _____ and heal him/her. This I ask in Jesus' Name.

Dear God,

I forgive myself for abusing my body by over-indulging it with food, stress, and caring for others. I will live a balanced life and honor my God-given gift. In Jesus' Name. Amen.

Dear God,

Forgive me for over working and burning the candle at both ends to achieve my personal goals. Help me to be content in the things You've already allowed me to achieve. I now honor my life by enjoying that which I have. Thank You Lord. In Jesus' Name. Amen.

Women's Prayers of Forgiveness
by Helen Orme

Dear God,
    I forgive myself for over-functioning and working beyond my limits. I now give myself permission to honor myself by engaging in daily intentional self-care. In Jesus' name. Amen.

Dear God,
    I forgive myself for abusing my body by over-indulging it with food, stress, and caring for others. I will live a balanced life and honor my God-given gift. In Jesus' name. Amen.

Dear God,
    I ask that you forgive me for not loving my body and esteeming my well-being. I ask that you grant unto me a greater appreciation of self. In Jesus' name. Amen.

Dear God,
    I forgive myself for all of the bad choices I've made in allowing others and myself to violate my dreams, goals, aspirations, and purpose. I now forgive them and myself. I forge forward into my destiny. In Jesus' name. Amen.

Dear God,
    I confess, I've allowed the expectations, disapproval, and rejections of others to define who I am. I now step out of the arena of failure, into the arena of success. I am who You say I am. In Jesus' name. Amen.

Dear God,

I forgive those who have violated me with harsh criticism, unfair treatment, and emotional, physical, and verbal abuse. Their tongues were like honey, but war was in their hearts. I pray for their wellbeing and for their lives to be transformed. In Jesus' name. Amen.

Dear God,

I forgive myself for holding on too tight and not letting go of things I have no control of, and things that were unhealthy. In Jesus' name. Amen.

Jesus Paid It All, Debts I Owe

Owe no man anything, but to love one another:
for he that loveth another hath fulfilled the law.
Romans 13:8

WRITE DOWN THE DEBT YOU OWE:
(Ex. The person you should show more love and appreciation to or the person who owes you)

1.

2.

3.

4.

5.

6.

7.

List ways in which you can begin to show more love or ways you would like to be shown appreciation:

1.

2.

3.

4.

5.

6.

7.

CONFESSION ONTO THE LORD

I CONFESS I'VE:

Who Am I: (Write down a paragraph about yourself)

What I like:

1.

2.

3.

4.

5.

What makes you happy?

1.

2.

3.

4.

5.

List the things that bring you great joy and a big smile to your face?

1.

2.

3.

4.

5.

List your hobbies:

1.

2.

3.

4.

5.

List the hobbies you would like to do:

1.

2.

3.

4.

5.

List your gifts and talents (also, skills and abilities)

1.

2.

3.

4.

5.

Things I do not like:

1.

2.

3.

4.

5.

Take a moment and dream without money: write down your heart's desires. Don't worry about the cost or skills or the ability to bring it to pass. Get pictures of things you would like to do, own, or visit and paste them into this section. (Read John 16:23)

Create a Personal Statement: (a statement describing you, your passion and your dream)

REMEMBER TO TELL YOURSELF:
"I have to love me in order to love you"

Take a moment to attend to you . . . it's the small things that count. Take a five minute sabbatical pause or an entire day alone, take a longer bath or go to the spa. Repeat as you do so: *"I have to attend to me in order to attend to you."*

List five things you will begin to do to take better care for yourself:

1.

2.

3.

4.

5.

After ministering/serving how do your replenish?

Spiritually:

Physically:

Emotionally:

Celebration

I will celebrate my success by:

_____

_____

_____

_____

_____

_____

_____

_____

_____

_____

_____

_____

_____

_____

_____

Nurture

<u>Nurture:</u>

I Need: _____

I Need: _____

I Need: _____

I Need: _____

I Need: _____

I Need: _____

I Need: _____

I Need: _____

I Need: _____

I Need: _____

Manifestation

Action Steps:

1.

2.

3.

4.

5.

6.

7.

8.

9.

10.

Affirmation:

I AM Statement:

I am: _____

I am: _____

I am: _____

I am: _____

I am: _____

I am: _____

I am: _____

I am: _____

I am: _____

I am: _____

Get It Out of You!!

Write down your goals for the next five years

Personal Goals:

1.

2.

3.

4.

5.

Professional/Career Goals

1.

2.

3.

4.

5.

SELF-CARE THROUGH PRAYER AND FORGIVENESS

. . . And it shall be forgiven . . . Leviticus 6:7

SELF-CARE THROUGH PRAYER AND FORGIVENESS

. . . And it shall be forgiven . . . Leviticus 6:7

_____

_____

_____

_____

_____

_____

_____

_____

_____

_____

_____

_____

_____

_____

SELF-CARE THROUGH PRAYER AND FORGIVENESS

. . . And it shall be forgiven . . . Leviticus 6:7

_____

_____

_____

_____

_____

_____

_____

_____

_____

_____

_____

_____

_____

_____

_____

_____

_____

SELF-CARE THROUGH PRAYER AND FORGIVENESS

. . . And it shall be forgiven . . . Leviticus 6:7

_____

_____

_____

_____

_____

_____

_____

_____

_____

_____

_____

_____

_____

_____

_____

_____

SELF-CARE THROUGH PRAYER AND FORGIVENESS

. . . And it shall be forgiven . . . Leviticus 6:7

_____

_____

_____

_____

_____

_____

_____

_____

_____

_____

_____

_____

_____

_____

_____

SELF-CARE THROUGH PRAYER AND FORGIVENESS

. . . And it shall be forgiven . . . Leviticus 6:7

_____

_____

_____

_____

_____

_____

_____

_____

_____

_____

_____

_____

_____

_____

_____

_____

SELF-CARE THROUGH PRAYER AND FORGIVENESS

. . . And it shall be forgiven . . . Leviticus 6:7

SELF-CARE THROUGH PRAYER AND FORGIVENESS

. . . And it shall be forgiven . . . Leviticus 6:7

_____

_____

_____

_____

_____

_____

_____

_____

_____

_____

_____

_____

_____

_____

_____

_____

SELF-CARE THROUGH PRAYER AND FORGIVENESS

. . . And it shall be forgiven . . . Leviticus 6:7

_____

_____

_____

_____

_____

_____

_____

_____

_____

_____

_____

_____

_____

_____

_____

_____

_____

SELF-CARE THROUGH PRAYER AND FORGIVENESS

. . . And it shall be forgiven . . . Leviticus 6:7

_____

_____

_____

_____

_____

_____

_____

_____

_____

_____

_____

_____

_____

_____

_____

_____

Daughters of Destiny' Affirmation

"Sing and rejoice, O daughter of Zion; for, lo I come and I will dwell in the midst of thee saith the Lord," Zech. 2:10

I walk as a Daughter of God

I walk as a Daughter with a Sound Mind and Love

I walk as a Daughter with Power

I walk as a Daughter of Integrity

I walk as a Daughter of Purpose

I walk as a Daughter of Destiny

I talk as a Daughter of God

I talk as a Daughter with a Sound Mind and Love

I talk as a Daughter with Power

I talk as a Daughter of Integrity

I talk as a Daughter of Purpose

I talk as a Daughter of Destiny

For I am a Daughter of God

For I am a Daughter with a Sound Mind and Love

For I am a Daughter with Power

For I am a Daughter of Integrity

For I am a Daughter of Purpose

For I am a Daughter of Destiny

"Women of God are Destined to be Blessed"
Helen Orme

"I Am Who I Am"

I am a Woman of Excellence

I am a Woman of Good Courage

I am a Woman of Integrity

I am a Woman of Loving Kindness

I am a Woman of Grace

I am a Woman of Knowledge

I am a Woman of Strength

I am a Woman of Greatness

I am a Beautiful Woman

I am a Triumphing Woman

I am a Blessed Woman

"I AM WHO GOD SAID I AM"

— Helen Orme

I RELEASE THE WOMAN INSIDE OF YOU TO
SOAR LIKE AN EAGLE INTO NEW HEIGHTS AND
DEEPER DEPTHS IN GOD.

"I pray that God will divinely Touch You Today."

Scriptures Regarding
Forgiveness of Enemies

Ex. 23:4. *If thou meet thine enemy's ox or his ass going astray, thou shalt surely bring it back to him again. 5. If thou see the ass of him that hateth thee lying under his burden, and wouldest forbear to help him, thou shalt surely help him.*

Prov. 19:11. *The discretion of a man deferreth his anger: and it is his glory to pass over a transgression.*

Prov. 24:17. *Rejoice not when thine enemy falleth, and let not thine heart be glad when he stumbleth: 29. Say not, I will do so to him as he hath done to me: I will render to the man according to his work.*

Prov. 25:21. *If thine enemy be hungry, give him bread to eat: and if he be thirsty, give him water to drink: 22. For thou shalt heap coals of fire upon his head, and the LORD shall reward thee. Rom. 12:20.*

Eccl. 7:21. *Take no heed unto all words that are spoken; lest thou hear thy servant curse thee:*

Matt. 5:7;39-46. *Blessed are the merciful: for they shall obtain mercy. 39. Resist not evil: but whosoever shall smite thee on thy right cheek, turn to him the other also. 40. And if any man will sue thee at the law, and take away thy coat, let him have thy cloke also. 41. And whosoever shall compel thee to go a mile, go with him twain. 43. It hath been said, Thou shalt love thy neighbour, and hate thine enemy. 44. But I say unto you, Love your enemies, bless them that curse you, do good to them that hate you, and pray for them which despitefully use you, and persecute you; 45. That ye may be the children of your Father, which is in heaven: for He maketh his sun to rise on the evil and on the good, and sendeth rain on the just and on the unjust. 46. For if ye love them which love you, what reward have ye? Do not even the publicans the same? 47. And if ye salute your brethren only, what do ye more than others? Do not even the publican so? 48. Be ye therefore perfect, even as your Father which is in heaven is perfect.*

Matt. 6:12-15. *Forgive us our debts, as we forgive our debtors. [Luke 11:4]. 14. If ye forgive men their trespasses, your heavenly Father will also forgive you: 15. But if ye forgive not men their trespasses, neither will your Father forgive your trespasses.*

Matt. 18:21-35. *Then came Peter to him, and said, Lord, how oft shall my brother sin against me, and I forgive him? Till seven times? 22. Jesus saith unto him, I say not unto thee, until seven times: but, until seventy times seven. 23. Therefore is the kingdom of heaven likened unto a certain king, which would take account of his servants. 24. And when he had begun to reckon, one was brought unto him, which owed him ten thousand talents. 25. But forasmuch as he had not to pay, his lord commanded him to be sold, and his wife, and children, and all that he had, and payment to be made. 26. The servant therefore fell down, and worshipped him, saying, Lord, have patience with me, and I will pay thee all. 27. Then the lord of that servant was moved with compassion, and loosed him, and forgave him the debt. 28. But the same servant went out, and found one of his fellow servants, which owed him an hundred pence: and he laid hands on him, and took him by the throat, saying, Pay me that thou owest. 29. And his fellow servant fell down at his feet, and besought him, saying, have patience with me, and I will pay thee all. 30. And he would not: but went and cast him into prison, till he should pay the debt. 31. So when his fellow servants saw what was done, they were very sorry, and came and told unto their lord all that was done. 32. Then his lord, after that he had called him, said unto him, O thou wicked servant, I forgave thee all that debt, because thou desiredst me: 33. Shouldest not thou also have had compassion on thy fellow servant, even as I had pity on thee? 34. And his lord was wroth, and delivered him to the tormentors, till he should pay all that was due unto him. 35. So likewise shall my heavenly Father do also unto you, if ye from your hearts forgive not everyone his brother their trespasses.*

Mark 11:25. *When ye stand praying forgive, if ye have ought against any: that your Father also which is in heaven may forgive you your trespasses.*

Luke 6:27-37. *27. But I say unto you which hear, Love your enemies, do good to them which hate you, 28. Bless them that curse you, and pray for them which despitefully use you. 29. And unto him that smiteth thee on the one cheek offer also the other; and him that taketh away thy cloke forbid not take thy coat also. Give to every man that asketh of thee; and of him that taketh away thy goods ask them not again. 31. And as ye would that men should do to you, do ye also to them likewise. 32. For if ye love them which love you, what thank have ye? For sinners also love those that love them. 33. And if ye do good to them which do good to you, what thank have ye? for sinners also do even the same. 34. And if ye lend to them of whom ye hope to receive, what thank have ye? for sinners also lend to sinners, to receive as much again. 35. But, love ye your enemies, and do good and lend, hoping for nothing again: and your reward shall be great, and ye shall be the children of the Highest: for he is kind unto the unthankful and to the evil. 36. Be ye therefore merciful, as your Father also is merciful. 37. Judge not, and ye shall not be judged: condemn not, and ye shall not be condemned: forgive, and ye shall be forgiven:*

Luke 17:3-4. *Take heed to yourselves: If thy brother trespass against thee, rebuke him: and if he repent, forgive him. 4. And if he trespass against thee seven times in a day, and seven times in a day turn again to thee, saying, I repent: thou shalt forgive him.* Matt. 18: 21, 22.

Rom. 12:14-21. *Bless them which persecute you: bless, and curse not. 17. Recompense to no man evil for evil . . . 19 . . . Avenge not yourselves, but rather, give place unto wrath: for it is written, Vengeance is mine: I will repay, saith the Lord. 21. Be not overcome of evil, but overcome evil with good.*

I Cor. 4:12-13. *Being reviled, we bless: being persecuted, we suffer it: 13. Being defamed, we intreat.*

Eph. 4:32. *Be ye kind one to another, tenderhearted, forgiving one another, even as God for Christ's sake hath forgiven you.*

Col. 3:13. *Forbearing one another, and forgiving one another, if any man have a quarrel against any: even as Christ forgave you so also do ye.*

Phil. 1:10-18. *I beseech thee for my son Onesimus . . . 18. If he hath wronged thee, or oweth thee ought, put that on mine account;*

I Pet. 3:9. *Not rendering evil for evil, or railing for railing: but contrariwise blessing; knowing that ye are thereunto called that ye should inherit a blessing.*

Instances of: Esau forgives Jacob, Gen. 33:4, 11. Joseph, forgives his brethren, Gen. 45:5-15: 50:19-21. Moses, forgives the Israelites, Num. 12:1-13; David forgives Saul, I Sam. 24:10-12; 26:9, 23; 2 Sam. 1:14-17; and Shimei, 2 Sam. 16:9-13; 19:23, with 1 Kin. 2:8,9. Solomon forgives Adonijah, 1 Kin. 1:52. The prophet of Judah forgives Jeroboam, 1 Kin. 13:3-6, Jesus forgives his enemies, Luke 23:34.

Scriptures Regarding Forgiveness

Psalm 130:4
But there is forgiveness with thee, that thou mayest be feared.

Daniel 9:9
To the Lord our God belong mercies and forgivenesses, though we have rebelled against him;

Mark 3:29
But he that shall blaspheme against the Holy Ghost hath never forgiveness, but is in danger of eternal damnation.

Acts 5:31
Him hath God exalted with his right hand to be a Prince and a Saviour, for to give repentance to Israel, and forgiveness of sins.

Acts 13:38
Be it known unto you therefore, men and brethren, that through this man is preached unto you the forgiveness of sins:

Acts 26:18
To open their eyes, and to turn them from darkness to light, and from the power of Satan unto God, that they may receive forgiveness of sins, and inheritance among them which are sanctified by faith that is in me.

Ephesians 1:7
In whom we have redemption through his blood, the forgiveness of sins, according to the riches of his grace;

Colossians 1:14
In whom we have redemption through his blood, even the forgiveness of sins:

Matthew 6:15
But if ye forgive not men their trespasses, neither will your Father forgive your trespasses.

Matthew 9:2
And, behold, they brought to him a man sick of the palsy, lying on a bed: and Jesus seeing their faith said unto the sick of the palsy; Son, be of good cheer; thy sins be forgiven thee.

Matthew 9:5
For whether is easier, to say, Thy sins be forgiven thee; or to say, Arise, and walk?

Matthew 9:6
But that ye may know that the Son of man hath power on earth to forgive sins, (then saith he to the sick of the palsy,) Arise, take up thy bed, and go unto thine house.

Matthew 12:31
Wherefore I say unto you, all manner of sin and blasphemy shall be forgiven unto men: but the blasphemy against the Holy Ghost shall not be forgiven unto men.

Matthew 12:32
And whosoever speaketh a word against the Son of man, it shall be forgiven him: but whosoever speaketh against the Holy Ghost, it shall not be forgiven him, neither in this world, neither in the world to come.

Matthew 18:21
Then came Peter to him, and said, Lord, how oft shall my brother sin against me, and I forgive him? Till seven times?

Matthew 18:35
So likewise shall my heavenly Father do also unto you, if ye from your hearts forgive not everyone his brother their trespasses.

Mark 2:5

When Jesus saw their faith, he said unto the sick of the palsy, Son, thy sins be forgiven thee.

Mark 2:7

Why doth this man thus speak blasphemies? Who can forgive sins but God only?

Mark 2:9

Whether is it easier to say to the sick of the palsy, Thy sins be forgiven thee; or to say, Arise, and take up thy bed, and walk?

Mark 2:10

But that ye may know that the Son of man hath power on earth to forgive sins, (he saith to the sick of the palsy,)

Mark 3:28

Verily I say unto you, All sins shall be forgiven unto the sons of men, and blasphemies wherewith soever they shall blaspheme:

Mark 3:29

But he that shall blaspheme against the Holy Ghost hath never forgiveness, but is in danger of eternal damnation.

Mark 4:12

That seeing they may see, and not perceive; and hearing they may hear, and not understand; lest at any time they should be converted, and their sins should be forgiven them.

Mark 11:25

And when ye stand praying, forgive, if ye have ought against any: that your Father also which is in heaven may forgive you your trespasses.

Mark 11:26

But if ye do not forgive, neither will your Father which is in heaven forgive your trespasses.

Luke 5:20

And when he saw their faith, he said unto him, Man, thy sins are forgiven thee.

Luke 5:21
And the scribes and the Pharisees began to reason, saying, Who is this which speaketh blasphemies? Who can forgive sins, but God alone?

Luke 5:23
Whether is easier, to say, Thy sins be forgiven thee; or to say, Rise up and walk?

Luke 5:24
But that ye may know that the Son of man hath power upon earth to forgive sins, (he said unto the sick of the palsy,) I say unto thee, Arise, and take up thy couch, and go into thine house.

Luke 6:37
Judge not, and ye shall not be judged: condemn not, and ye shall not be condemned: forgive, and ye shall be forgiven:

Luke 7:47
Wherefore I say unto thee, Her sins, which are many, are forgiven; for she loved much: but to whom little is forgiven, the same loveth little.

Luke 7:48
And he said unto her, Thy sins are forgiven.

Luke 7:49
And they that sat at meat with him began to say within themselves, Who is this that forgiveth sins also?

Luke 11:4
And forgive us our sins; for we also forgive every one that is indebted to us. And lead us not into temptation; but deliver us from evil.

Luke 12:10
And whosoever shall speak a word against the Son of man, it shall be forgiven him: but unto him that blasphemeth against the Holy Ghost it shall not be forgiven.

Luke 17:3
Take heed to yourselves: If thy brother trespass against thee, rebuke him; and if he repent, forgive him.

Luke 17:4
And if he trespass against thee seven times in a day, and seven times in a day turn again to thee, saying, I repent; thou shalt forgive him.

Luke 23:34
Then said Jesus, Father, forgive them; for they know not what they do. And they parted his raiment, and cast lots.

Acts 5:31
Him hath God exalted with his right hand to be a Prince and a Saviour, for to give repentance to Israel, and forgiveness of sins.

Acts 8:22
Repent therefore of this thy wickedness, and pray God, if perhaps the thought of thine heart may be forgiven thee.

Acts 13:38
Be it known unto you therefore, men and brethren, that through this man is preached unto you the forgiveness of sins:

Acts 26:18
To open their eyes, and to turn them from darkness to light, and from the power of Satan unto God, that they may receive forgiveness of sins, and inheritance among them which are sanctified by faith that is in me.

Romans 4:7
Saying, Blessed are they whose iniquities are forgiven, and whose sins are covered.

2 Corinthians 2:7
So that contrariwise ye ought rather to forgive him, and comfort him, lest perhaps such a one should be swallowed up with overmuch sorrow.

2 Corinthians 2:10
To whom ye forgive anything, I forgive also: for if I forgave anything, to whom I forgave it, for your sakes forgave I it in the person of Christ;

2 Corinthians 12:13
For what is it wherein ye were inferior to other churches, except it be that I myself was not burdensome to you? forgive me this wrong.

Ephesians 1:7
    In whom we have redemption through his blood, the forgiveness of sins, according to the riches of his grace;

Ephesians 4:32
    And be ye kind one to another, tenderhearted, forgiving one another, even as God for Christ's sake hath forgiven you.

Colossians 1:14
    In whom we have redemption through his blood, even the forgiveness of sins:

Colossians 2:13
    And you, being dead in your sins and the uncircumcision of your flesh, hath he quickened together with him, having forgiven you all trespasses;

James 5:15
    And the prayer of faith shall save the sick, and the Lord shall raise him up; and if he have committed sins, they shall be forgiven him.

1 John 1:9
    If we confess our sins, he is faithful and just to forgive us our sins, and to cleanse us from all unrighteousness.

1 John 2:12
    I write unto you, little children, because your sins are forgiven you for his name's sake.

Scriptures Regarding Prayer

Psalm 102:1
> Hear my prayer, O LORD, and let my cry come unto thee.

Psalm 102:17
> He will regard the prayer of the destitute, and not despise their prayer.

Psalm 109:4
> For my love they are my adversaries: but I give myself unto prayer.

Psalm 109:7
> When he shall be judged, let him be condemned: and let his prayer become sin.

Psalm 141:2
> Let my prayer be set forth before thee as incense; and the lifting up of my hands as the evening sacrifice.

Psalm 141:5
> Let the righteous smite me; it shall be a kindness: and let him reprove me; it shall be an excellent oil, which shall not break my head: for yet my prayer also shall be in their calamities.

Psalm 143:1
> Hear my prayer, O LORD, give ear to my supplications: in thy faithfulness answer me, and in thy righteousness.

Proverbs 15:8
> The sacrifice of the wicked is an abomination to the LORD: but the prayer of the upright is his delight.

Proverbs 15:29

The LORD is far from the wicked: but he heareth the prayer of the righteous.

Proverbs 28:9

He that turneth away his ear from hearing the law, even his prayer shall be abomination.

Isaiah 1:15

And when ye spread forth your hands, I will hide mine eyes from you: yea, when ye make many prayers, I will not hear: your hands are full of blood.

Isaiah 26:16

LORD, in trouble have they visited thee, they poured out a prayer when thy chastening was upon them.

Isaiah 37:4

It may be the LORD thy God will hear the words of Rabshakeh, whom the king of Assyria his master hath sent to reproach the living God, and will reprove the words which the LORD thy God hath heard: wherefore lift up thy prayer for the remnant that is left.

Isaiah 38:5

Go, and say to Hezekiah, Thus saith the LORD, the God of David thy father, I have heard thy prayer, I have seen thy tears: behold, I will add unto thy days fifteen years.

Isaiah 56:7

Even them will I bring to my holy mountain, and make them joyful in my house of prayer: their burnt offerings and their sacrifices shall be accepted upon mine altar; for mine house shall be called an house of prayer for all people.

Jeremiah 7:16

Therefore pray not thou for this people, neither lift up cry nor prayer for them, neither make intercession to me: for I will not hear thee.

Jeremiah 11:14

Therefore pray not thou for this people, neither lift up a cry or prayer for them: for I will not hear them in the time that they cry unto me for their trouble.

Lamentations 3:8
  Also when I cry and shout, he shutteth out my prayer.

Lamentations 3:44
  Thou hast covered thyself with a cloud, that our prayer should not pass through.

Daniel 9:3
  And I set my face unto the Lord God, to seek by prayer and supplications, with fasting, and sackcloth, and ashes:

Daniel 9:13
  As it is written in the law of Moses, all this evil is come upon us: yet made we not our prayer before the LORD our God, that we might turn from our iniquities, and understand thy truth.

Daniel 9:17
  Now therefore, O our God, hear the prayer of thy servant, and his supplications, and cause thy face to shine upon thy sanctuary that is desolate, for the Lord's sake.

Daniel 9:21
  Yea, whiles I was speaking in prayer, even the man Gabriel, whom I had seen in the vision at the beginning, being caused to fly swiftly, touched me about the time of the evening oblation.

Jonah 2:7
  When my soul fainted within me I remembered the LORD: and my prayer came in unto thee, into thine holy temple.

Matthew 17:21
  Howbeit this kind goeth not out but by prayer and fasting.

Matthew 21:13
  And said unto them, It is written, My house shall be called the house of prayer; but ye have made it a den of thieves.

Matthew 21:22
  And all things, whatsoever ye shall ask in prayer, believing, ye shall receive.

Matthew 23:14

    Woe unto you, scribes and Pharisees, hypocrites! for ye devour widows' houses, and for a pretence make long prayer: therefore ye shall receive the greater damnation.

Mark 9:29

    And he said unto them, This kind can come forth by nothing, but by prayer and fasting.

Mark 11:17

    And he taught, saying unto them, Is it not written, My house shall be called of all nations the house of prayer? but ye have made it a den of thieves.

Mark 12:40

    Which devour widows' houses, and for a pretence make long prayers: these shall receive greater damnation.

Luke 1:13

    But the angel said unto him, Fear not, Zacharias: for thy prayer is heard; and thy wife Elisabeth shall bear thee a son, and thou shalt call his name John.

Luke 2:37

    And she was a widow of about fourscore and four years, which departed not from the temple, but served God with fastings and prayers night and day.

Luke 5:33

    And they said unto him, Why do the disciples of John fast often, and make prayers, and likewise the disciples of the Pharisees; but thine eat and drink?

Luke 6:12

    And it came to pass in those days, that he went out into a mountain to pray, and continued all night in prayer to God.

Luke 19:46

    Saying unto them, It is written, My house is the house of prayer: but ye have made it a den of thieves.

Luke 20:47

    Which devour widows' houses, and for a shew make long prayers: the same shall receive greater damnation.

Luke 22:45

And when he rose up from prayer, and was come to his disciples, he found them sleeping for sorrow,

Acts 1:14

These all continued with one accord in prayer and supplication, with the women, and Mary the mother of Jesus, and with his brethren.

Acts 2:42

And they continued stedfastly in the apostles' doctrine and fellowship, and in breaking of bread, and in prayers.

Acts 3:1

Now Peter and John went up together into the temple at the hour of prayer, being the ninth hour.

Acts 6:4

But we will give ourselves continually to prayer, and to the ministry of the word.

Acts 10:4

And when he looked on him, he was afraid, and said, What is it, Lord? And he said unto him, Thy prayers and thine alms are come up for a memorial before God.

Acts 10:31

And said, Cornelius, thy prayer is heard, and thine alms are had in remembrance in the sight of God.

Acts 12:5

Peter therefore was kept in prison: but prayer was made without ceasing of the church unto God for him.

Acts 16:13

And on the sabbath we went out of the city by a river side, where prayer was wont to be made; and we sat down, and spake unto the women which resorted thither.

Acts 16:16

And it came to pass, as we went to prayer, a certain damsel possessed with a spirit of divination met us, which brought her masters much gain by soothsaying:

Romans 1:9

For God is my witness, whom I serve with my spirit in the gospel of his Son, that without ceasing I make mention of you always in my prayers;

Romans 10:1

Brethren, my heart's desire and prayer to God for Israel is, that they might be saved.

Appendix A

LESSON ON THE GREAT SAYING OF JESUS FORGIVENESS

Lesson Text:
Matthew 18:21-35

21 Then came Peter to him, and said, Lord, how oft shall my brother sin against me, and I forgive him? Till seven times?

22 Jesus saith unto him, I say not unto thee, until seven times: but, until seventy times seven.

23 Therefore is the kingdom of heaven likened unto a certain king, which would take account of his servants.

24 And when he had begun to reckon, one was brought unto him, which owed him ten thousand talents.

25 But forasmuch as he had not to pay, his lord commanded him to be sold, and his wife, and children, and all that he had, and payment to be made.

26 The servant therefore fell down, and worshipped him, saying, Lord, have patience with me, and I will pay thee all.

27 Then the Lord of that servant was moved with compassion, and loosed him, and forgave him the debt.

28 But the same servant went out, and found one of his fellow servants, which owed him an hundred pence: and he laid hands on him, and took him by the throat, saying, Pay me that thou owest.

29 And his fellow servant fell down at his feet, and besought him, saying Have patience with me, and I will pay thee all.

30 And he would not: but went and cast him into prison, till he should pay the debt.

31 So when his fellows servants saw what was done, they were very sorry, and came and told unto their lord all that was done.

32 Then his lord, after that he had called him, said unto him, O thou wicked servant, I forgave thee all that debt, because thou desiredest me:

33 Shouldest not thou also have had compassion on thy fellow servant, even as I have pity on thee?

34 And his lord was worth, and delivered him to the tormentors, till he should pay all that was due unto him.

35 So likewise shall my heavenly Father do also unto you, if ye from your hearts forgive not everyone his brother their trespasses.

Lesson Outline

Introduction

  I. Seeking Forgiveness from God
     A. Recognize the Need for Forgiveness
     B. Repent of Wrongdoing
  II. Receiving Forgiveness
     A. Removes Condemnation
     B. Brings Freedom from Sin
  II. Extending Forgiveness
     A. Forgive to Be Forgiven
     B. Leave Vengeance to God
     C. God's Love Is Shown in His Forgiveness of Our Sins
     D. We Love God Because He First Loved Us
     E. Continue to Forgive

Conclusion

Reflections

INTRODUCTION

The idea of forgiveness is linked to the story of mankind. When Adam and Eve disobeyed God and ate fruit from the forbidden tree, they discovered the disciplinary side of God. As punishment for their wrongdoing, God removed them from the idyllic setting of Eden into a world of struggles, sweat, and death.

> *Unto the woman he said, I will greatly multiply thy sorrow and thy conception; in sorrow thou shalt bring forth children; and thy desire shall be to thy husband and he shall rule over thee. And unto Adam he said, Because thou hast hearkened unto the voice of thy wife, and hast eaten of the tree, of which I commanded thee, saying, Thou shalt not eat of it: cursed is the ground for thy sake: in sorrow shalt thou eat of it all the days of thy life; thorns also and thistles shall it bring forth to thee; and thus shalt eat the herb of the field; in the sweat of thy face shalt thou eat bread, till thou return unto the ground; for out of it wast thou taken; for dust thou art, and unto dust shalt thou return . . . Therefore the Lord God sent him forth from the garden of Eden, to till the ground from whence he was taken."* (Genesis 3:16-19, 23).

Their punishment actually was less than what they deserved. God had warned Adam that to disobey would cause death. Death came in two ways when Adam and Eve disobeyed: (1) they suffered immediate, spiritual death, which severed their intimate relationship with God in the Garden; and (2) they began the process of aging, which eventually culminated in their physical death. Mercifully, however, God permitted Adam to live 930 years before he died physically.

God's mercy is the principle upon which the doctrine of forgiveness is built. God has always punished and always will punish those who commit sin. Because wrongdoing is contrary to God's nature and He abhors it, he punishes those who commit it. Yet, He also makes provision for sinners to be relieved from the penalty of their transgressions by making a way for them to receive forgiveness. In Adam and Eve's case, he granted them many more years of life, provided them with clothing, and gave them a promise that one of their offspring would take vengeance upon the serpentine adversary of their souls.

Through Moses, God provided a working solution to the sin-imposed guilt of the Hebrews-atonement through blood sacrifices. For almost two thousand years, from Moses to Jesus Christ, the blood of animal sacrifices brought divine pardon and forgiveness for sin by looking forward to the redemptive death of Christ on the cross. Jesus took the place of the sacrificial lambs, and as the Lamb of God, He dealt with the sins of the world.

John the Baptist declared the identity of Jesus when he stated, "Behold the Lamb of God, which taketh away the sin of the world" (John 1:29). Jesus' sacrificial death on Calvary wonderfully provides forgiveness for the sins of mankind and restores the broken relationship with God, but His act of forgiveness also calls upon human beings to make amends for their wrongful deeds committed against one another. Personal affronts and hurt require personal forgiveness to restore the horizontal relationship between estranged individuals.

Jesus taught that divine forgiveness is built upon divine mercy. Divine mercy is the unmerited favor that forgives the sin and the person committing it. He also taught that those who refuse to show mercy to others—by refusing to forgive them—disqualify themselves from receiving the mercy and forgiveness of God. The unforgiving will be the unforgiven. "For if ye forgive men their trespasses, your heavenly Father will also forgive you; but if ye forgive not men their trespasses, neither will your Father forgive your trespasses" (Matthew 6:14-15).

I. SEEKING FORGIVENESS FROM GOD

The process of seeking forgiveness begins in the mind and moves to the heart. Awareness of sin and wrongdoing begins first in our minds. We mentally recognize the fact of our misdeeds; however, only admitting what we have done wrong is insufficient to bring about forgiveness from God and those whom we have offended. Some people acknowledge their sins but then rationalize them away. In an attempt to explain away their misdeeds as part of a universal problem, they quote Romans 3:23: "For all have sinned, and come short of the glory of God." They ask, "Since everyone sins, what's the big deal? What difference does it make?" They stop short of actually being sorrowful or repentant, wrongly thinking that to acknowledge their mistakes is enough. But admission alone is inadequate.

A. Recognize the Need for Forgiveness

Forgiveness depends on more than mentally acknowledging wrongdoing. It requires an emotional response of sorrow. The Bible declares that it is impossible for God to forgive an unremorseful or unrepentant person. Sorrow on the part of the wrongdoer must precede forgiveness. Without remorse for sins, there is no true sense of wrongdoing and the harm it has caused. The apostle Paul provided some insights into the powerful emotions that accompany true godly sorrow, repentance, and forgiveness.

> *"For though I made you sorry with a letter, I do not repent, though I did repent; for I perceive that the same epistle hath made you sorry, though it were but for a season. Now I rejoice, not that ye were made sorry, but that ye sorrowed to repentance; for ye were made sorry after a godly manner, that ye might receive damage by us in nothing. For godly sorrow worketh repentance to salvation not to be repented of: but the sorrow of the world worketh death. For behold this selfsame thing, that ye sorrowed after a godly sort, what carefulness it wrought in you, yea, what clearing of yourselves, yea, what indignation, yea, what fear, yea, what vehement desire, yea, what zeal, yea, what revenge! In all things ye have approved yourselves to be clear in this matter"* (II Corinthians 7:8-11).

B. Repent of Wrongdoing

The motivation for true repentance comes from acknowledging the damage and hurts caused by the wrongs one has committed, a genuine sorrow for the wrongs done, and a sincere desire to undo the damages they have caused. True repentance leads a person both to recognize that something is terribly wrong and to desire to be restored to right standing with God and one's fellow man. He desires to rid himself of the guilt and shame he suffers from his wrongdoing.

Sin broke the relationship between Adam and God and, by extension, between all mankind and God. To restore the broken relationship, God requires true repentance. Moreover, repentance and forgiveness are possible only because of the supreme sacrifice of Jesus Christ made on the cross to atone for sins. Consequently, we must offer nothing less than true repentance. In return, God will give us true forgiveness!

II. Receiving Forgiveness

If God forgives, we must forgive ourselves. Otherwise it is almost like setting up ourselves as a higher tribunal than Him.

—C. S. Lewis (1898-1963)

To be complete, forgiveness must be offered, and it must be accepted. A person condemned to prison who receives a pardon must accept that pardon before he can be released. It is a strange fact that many Christians have never received the forgiveness of sins that God promises. They have acknowledged their sinful life, confessed their sins to God, and asked for His forgiveness through true repentance, but they have never accepted the forgiveness for which they asked. They still hold the guilt and condemnation of an unrepentant soul. For the grace of God to be effective, a believer must accept it.

> About the year 1830, a man named George Wilson killed a government employee who caught him in the act of robbing the mail. He was tried and sentenced to be hanged. However, President Andrew Jackson sent him a pardon, and no one knew what to do. So the case was carried to the Supreme Court of the United States.
>
> Chief Justice Marshall, perhaps one of the greatest justices ever, wrote the court's opinion. In it he said, "A pardon is a slip of paper, the value of which is determined by the acceptance of the person to be pardoned. If it is refused, it is no pardon. George Wilson must be hanged." And so he was.

A. Removes Condemnation

"There is therefore no condemnation to them who are in Christ Jesus, who walk not after the flesh, but after the Spirit" (Romans 8:1).

Receiving God's forgiveness removes the penalty of our sins and misdeeds. Forgiveness means that we no longer owe anything for wrongdoing. There is nothing more that can be, or needs to be, done to bring a feeling that all is well between God and us. Those who accept the forgiveness of sins are no longer under their penalty. Baptism in the name of Jesus Christ is the act by which all sins are once and forever forgiven, remitted, and forgotten. Acts 2:38 reveals how to remove the condemnation of sin: "Repent, and be baptized every one of you in the name of Jesus Christ for the remission of sins, and ye shall receive the gift of the Holy Ghost." When we receive God's forgiveness, all our past sins are forgiven and forgotten—forever.

> *"I, even I, am he that blotteth out thy transgressions for mine own sake, and will not remember thy sins"* (Isaiah 43:25).

> *"He hath not dealt with us after our sins; nor rewarded us according to our iniquities. For as the heaven is high above the earth, so great is his mercy toward them that fear him. As far as the east is from the west, so far hath he removed our transgression from us"* (Psalm 103:10-12).

It is a geological fact that the North Pole is a measured distance from the South Pole, but there is no way to measure the east from the west! That is the distance that psalmist stated that our sins have been removed from us! (See Psalm 103:12)

The prophet Micah described God's forgiveness as taking all our sins and casting them into the depths of the sea. (Micah 7:18-19). Further, some of the old hymns use that terminology to describe the joy that comes from having our sins pardoned.

> *Gone, gone, gone, gone, yes my sins have gone!*
> *Now my soul is free and in my heart's a song!*
> *Buried in the deepest sea, yes, that's good enough for me!*
> *I shall live eternally, praise God, my sins have gone!*
> —Helen Griggs, 1936

> *Down in the depths of the deepest sea,*
> *Lie all the sins once charged to me.*
> *Buried for time and eternity,*
> *Down in the deepest sea.*
> Norman J. Clayton, 1945

> *You ask me why I'm happy, so I'll just tell you why,*
> *Because my sins are gone!*

And when I meet the scoffers, who ask me where they are
I say, my sins are gone!
They're underneath the blood, on the cross of Calvary,
As far removed as darkness is from dawn;
In the sea of God's forgetfulness, that's good enough for me,
Praise God, my sins are gone!

—N. B. Vandall, 1934

God wants us to realize that the forgiveness He freely offers is complete and forever. When our sins are forgiven, they are forgotten. The past—with its sins, hurts, brokenness, and self-recrimination-is gone, dead, crucified, and remembered no more. What God forgives, He forgets!

B. Brings Freedom from Sin

"If the Son therefore shall make you free, ye shall be free indeed"
John 8:36

It is sad to note that many Christians have never found the liberty over sin that Jesus Christ promises. Despite being baptized in Jesus' name and speaking in tongues when receiving the Holy Spirit, some still are bound to old habits, attitudes, and ways of behaving. Rather than becoming "new creatures" in Christ (II Corinthians 5:17), they still are bound in fetters to the "old man" of the flesh (Colossian 3:9). This is definitely contrary to the will of God. The apostle Paul wrote, "Knowing this, that our old man is crucified with him, that the body of sin might be destroyed, that henceforth we should not serve sin. For he that is dead is freed from sin." (Romans 6:6-7).

Finding forgiveness provides freedom from the penalty of sin. Accepting forgiveness allows us to look ahead with hope of a heavenly reward rather than with a sense of dread of eternal punishment. Forgiveness also releases us to live sinlessly consecrated to God out of a sense of appreciation for what He has done. God's forgiveness means we no longer are captives-slaves to sin-but liberated, delivered, and set free to live a glorious life in Christ Jesus.

III. EXTENDING FORGIVENESS

Simon Wiesenthal was a prisoner and survivor of the Nazi concentration camps. After the war, he told the story of how, as the war was ending, he encountered a Nazi who made him listen to a confession of all the atrocities he had committed against Jews. The SS trooper told him he was tormented by guilt and begged Wiesenthal said, "That, I cannot do." Instead he turned and walked away. Later, Wiesenthal's own conscience began to bother him and he wondered if he had done the right thing in refusing to forgive the SS trooper.

In light of how God deals with our sins, how should we treat others who have wronged us? If someone is truly sorry and repents of his crimes and asks us for forgiveness, should we not forgive the person? Or are there some crimes that simply cannot be forgiven? Simon Peter approached Jesus on the subject of forgiveness. "Then came Peter to him, and said, Lord, how oft shall my brother sin against me, and I forgive him? Till seven times? Jesus saith unto him, I say not unto thee, until seven times: but, until seventy times seven" (Matthew 18:21-22).

When Peter asked Jesus how often a person should forgive, he thought that forgiving would be very generous. (See Luke 17:4) Jesus taught him a profound lesson. The different translators define Jesus' words as meaning either seventy-seven times or 490 times in one day, but the point remains the same in either case: forgiveness is not to be doled out in droplets, but in great running rivers of mercy!

A. Forgive to Be Forgiven

Following His conversation with Simon Peter about the number of times we should forgive others, Jesus shared the parable of the unforgiving servant. (See Matthew 18:23-35) It describes a man who, having been forgiven a great debt then refused to forgive another man a comparatively small debt owed to him. It provides a vivid picture of how God expects us to act toward those who have wronged us. We must forgive them. It is that simple. True repentance brings us forgiveness from God, and it should do the same for our fellow man.

Jesus taught that those who refuse to show mercy to others—by refusing to forgive them—disqualify themselves from receiving the mercy and forgiveness of God. The unforgiving person will be unforgiven. Jesus stated, "For if ye forgive men their trespasses, your heavenly Father will also forgive you: but if ye forgive not men their trespasses, neither will your Father forgive your trespasses" (Matthew 6:14-15). It is imperative that we forgive others. Our own salvation depends on our doing so.

B. Leave Vengeance to God

"Thou shalt not avenge, nor bear any grudge against the children of thy people, but thou shalt love thy neighbour as thyself: I am the Lord? (Leviticus 19:18).

"Dearly beloved, avenge not yourselves, but rather give place unto wrath; for it is written, Vengeance is mine; I will repay, saith the Lord" (Romans 12:19).

The Bible recognizes the basic human nature for a person to seek revenge for wrongs committed against him. Yet, God wants us to follow a more charitable way—loving and forgiving others, leaving all retribution and punishment to Him. He is just. Eventually, He will punish the wicked and reward the righteous.

Alexander C. Dejong (1922-2003), a noted seminarian, once gave these guidelines for dealing with forgiveness and vengeance: "To forgive someone involves three things. First, it means to forego the right of striking back. One rejects the urge to repay gossip with gossip and a bad turn with a worse turn. Second, it means replacing the feeling of resentment and anger with good will, a love which seeks the others welfare, not harm. Third, it means the forgiving person takes concrete steps to restore good relations."

Somehow in our desire to redress wrongs committed against us, we must restrain our human impulse to punish others. Only God can truly determine the motives of any person. Only He knows the true intent behind each thought and deed. What we might think was intentional on the part of others may have been done in ignorance or carelessness. Our viewpoints are limited, but His is perfect; we must turn all hurts over to Him for justice. That is not always an easy thing to do, but it is always the right thing to do.

C. God's Love Is Shown In His Forgiveness of Our Sins

"Herein is love, not that we loved God, but that he loved us, and sent his son to be the propitiation for our sins." (I John 4:10)

Jesus Christ was the "propitiation for our sins." Through His atoning death we are able to obtain the forgiveness of sins.

> "*Therefore by the deeds of the law there shall no flesh be justified in his sight: for by the law is the knowledge of sin. But now the righteousness of God without the law is manifested, being witnessed by the law and the prophets; Even the righteousness of God which is by faith of Jesus Christ unto all and upon all them that believe: for there is no difference: For all have sinned, and come short of the glory of God; Being justified freely by his grace through the redemption that is in Christ Jesus: Whom God hath set forth to be a propitiation through faith in his blood, to declare his righteousness for the remission of sins that are past, through the forbearance of God; To declare, I say, at this time his righteousness: that he might be just, and the justifier of him which believeth in Jesus. Where is boasting then? It is excluded. By what law? of works? Nay: but by the law of faith. Therefore we conclude that a man is justified by faith without the deeds of the law.* (Romans 3:20-28)

The law did not provide forgiveness, but what the law could not do, God accomplished by *"sending his own Son in the likeness of sinful flesh" (Romans 8:3)*. Many people feel unworthy of God's forgiveness, and their spiritual insecurity hinders their faith horribly. Many wail, "I've failed God so terribly." The truth is, "All have sinned, and come short of the glory of God" (Roman 3:23). The apostle Paul referred to himself as the worst of sinners and added that he obtained mercy "for a pattern to them which should hereafter believe on him to life everlasting" (I Timothy 1:16). If God would grant forgiveness to the "chief" of sinners, surely He would do it for anyone else. This gives every sinner hope for salvation through Christ's forgiveness of his sins.

The thief on the cross serves as an example of how forgiveness is available to all who turn to Jesus Christ in faith. (See Luke 23:39-43.) The thief had done nothing to merit God's mercy. He did not observe God's law; he was a thief! Yet, because he embraced the propitiatory death of Christ, Jesus forgave him. On this side of the cross, we must repent of our sins, be baptized in Jesus' name for the remission of sins, and receive the Holy Spirit, (Luke 24:46-40: Acts 2:38).

D. We Love God Because He First Loved Us

"We love him, because he first loved us" (I John 4:19).

God's love made forgiveness of sin possible. His love built a bridge over the gulf of our sins by which we are able to leave our sinful past behind through faith. (See Ephesians 2:8-9).

The death of Jesus Christ is the basis for our being able to experience His love and forgiveness (Romans 5:5). The love God demonstrated through the suffering and death of Jesus Christ paved the way for us to love Him. Without Christ's death, we would still be in bondage to sin, incapable of experiencing God's loving kindness, mercy and forgiveness.

E. Continue to Forgive

"Take heed to yourselves: if thy brother trespass against thee, rebuke him; and if he repent, forgive him. And if he trespass against thee seven times in a day, and seven times in a day turn again to thee, saying, I repent; thou shalt forgive him" (Luke 17:3-4).

> *Jesus taught that forgiveness is not just an once-in-a-lifetime event. Every person must practice forgiveness daily. The Lord's Prayer teaches us to say, "Give us this day our daily bread. And forgive us our debt as we forgive our debtors" (Matthew 6:11-12). This seems to equate our daily need for food to our daily need to forgive others. Moreover, it is possible that each of us hurts someone else every day, and we need to repent and receive forgiveness ourselves. We all need to follow the mandate of Scripture: Be slow to anger and quick to forgive.*

"Wherefore, my beloved brethren, let every man be swift to hear, slow to speak, slow to wrath: For the wrath of man worketh not the righteousness of God." *(James 1:19-20).*

CONCLUSION

Our lesson has focused on the fact that if we are to receive true forgiveness from God and others, we must be willing to forgive those who have wronged us. When we seek forgiveness from others, we must be motivated by an attitude of godly sorrow and a desire to restore fellowship.

Being forgiven is a liberating experience. And being forgiven of our sins brings us the freedom to live above them. However, each of us must practice the act of forgiving others on a daily basis in order to truly receive and benefit from God's forgiveness. Moreover, we must learn to leave all revenge and punishment in God's hands. Judgment and punishment are God's exclusive privilege and responsibility, not mankind's.

REFLECTIONS

- Discuss how sin affected Adam and Eve's relationship with God. What does sin do to our relationship with God? Discuss.
- The forgiveness of all sins looks to the supreme sacrifice of Jesus Christ on the cross. Discuss why John recognized and identified Him as "the Lamb of God."
- Discuss the relationship between extending forgiveness to others who have wronged us and receiving the forgiveness of God.
- Discuss the necessity of receiving God's forgiveness. Is it possible that God would offer forgiveness, but, because of guilt, we would fail to receive His forgiveness?
- What is the determined distance between the east and the west? Discuss why the psalmist stated that our sins have been removed from us as far as the east is from the west.

Appendix B

Therapy Prayer and Journaling

R. Scott Sullender, Ph.D.
Associate Professor of Pastoral Counseling
San Francisco Theological Seminary

Therapy can be an emotionally intense experience. You will become more aware of your pain—past or current pain. You will realize parts of yourself that had not previously been known or embraced. You will become more aware of your weaknesses and your gifts. You will pass through periods of confusion and anxiety, when you don't know who you are or where you are going. This is all a part of the process of therapy. When you come out on the other side, you'll be a stronger and wiser person, who is also more whole and more loving.

> *"I have so much to do that I must spend several hours in prayer before I am able to do it."*
>
> —John Wesley

A Companion on the Road Less Traveled

As you enter into a period of psychotherapy, we urge you to also enter into a period of regular prayer. Regardless of your religious tradition, we find that clients who have an active prayer life get more out of therapy. Their therapy moves faster and goes deeper.

Find yourself a regular time for prayer a quiet time in your day or week. Don't rush through your prayer. Take time to enjoy it, nourish it. Take

116

time to speak and listen in prayer. Use your prayer time to center yourself. Breathe deeply. Get in touch with the deepest parts of your soul. Listen to your soul. Listen to your love and your pain, your sorrow and joy, your anger and your peace.

Use your prayer time to reflect on the themes that are emerging in your therapy. Ask God to give you further insights and discernment regarding your therapeutic work. Push the boundaries of your awareness and your memory.

Use your prayer time for confession, as you come to see your shortcomings, failures and sins more clearly in therapy. Allow God to nurture you with forgiveness and grace.

Use your prayer time to ask God to walk with you, to be your companion in your process of self-exploration, and to give you discernment, courage and wisdom to make the tough decisions that come with your journey.

Use your prayer time to give thanks. Recall your blessings, especially the unseen blessings that arise out of sufferings.

Use your prayer time to remember the needs of others, lifting up their names in love. Say a word of prayer for people who do not like you or who have treated you badly. This will help them and release you of resentment.

Use your prayer time to listen, as well as speak. Pay attention to the thoughts that come into your mind and heart while in prayer, or those spoken to you through the voice of others soon after prayer times. Bring these "listening" with you to your next therapy session.

Prayer and Scripture

Many Christians like to practice a special discipline of prayer called "Praying the Scriptures." This discipline has been practiced in both Protestant and Catholic churches, although more closely associated with the Benedictine tradition.

Choose a Scripture passage. Read through it slowly, letting your awareness rest in turn upon each word, savoring it. Focus on any word or phrase that draws your attention. Meditate upon this word, phrase or situation. Allow it to connect with particular memories, words, feelings and images from your life. How does the Word touch your soul? How does your soul wish to respond to God's Word?

> *We are all wounded people . . . The God who lives within us will give us the grace to go beyond our wounded selves and say . . . "you are forgiven."*
>
> —Henri Nouwen

If the Scripture passage is a scene or story, place yourself in that story. Which character do you identify with? Or perhaps you are just an observer as the story unfolds? Imagine you are there. Notice the sights, sounds and smells. Imagine you are interacting with the characters of the passage. What happens? Pay attention to the feelings and thoughts that you have at each stage in this story. Embellish the story in your imagination.

How does God speak to you in and through this Scripture passage? Allow God's message to surround you, enfold you and bathe you in love. Respond to God and God's Word to you as you feel prompted. Perhaps you will feel moved to confession, thanksgiving, intercessory prayers or other responses.

If you need help finding appropriate Scripture passages, your therapist can suggest several.

Therapy and Journaling

Some clients prefer to "pray with a pen in their hand." They find the discipline of journaling to be very beneficial to them in general and as another companion with their therapy.

Do you like to write? Then journaling is for you

Begin by establishing a regular discipline time for journaling, daily or weekly. The instruction are simple: Write as the Spirit moves you. Write whatever comes to your mind—a dairy, or to God or to some special wise spiritual confidant. Begin with themes or insights that come out of your therapy sessions. Note the places in your day or week where those themes surfaced again. Push back the boundary of your awareness. Use this format to reveal information or memories that have yet been too difficult to speak out loud in a therapy session.

Unlike a diary this is not a travel log or an accounting of dates and activities. Journaling is a description of your soul's activity. It is an account of your inner life, not your outer life.

Some people like to also use Scripture as a starting point to their journaling.

Your therapist may also give you specific assignments or exercises to do in your journaling.

Some clients prefer to keep their journals private. Others prefer to bring them in to their next therapy session, reading segments that they want to discuss further. If your therapist is willing, some clients like to have their therapist read their journals prior to the next therapy session.

In Conclusion . . .

As we pass through painful and troubling periods, praying, like therapy may get difficult for a time. It is not uncommon for people of faith to have periods when it seems like God is distant. Earlier Christians called these periods "the dark night of the soul" or "the silence of God." If such times come we urge you to keep praying, and stay in therapy. Only by entering into the pain will you pass through it. Only by passing through "death" do we find "resurrection."

We want you to receive the most benefit possible from your therapy. We want you to find healing, forgiveness, guidance, understanding and acceptance.

It has been our experience that Prayer and Journaling are two excellent parallel disciplines to the process of Therapy. Done separately or together, they can enrich your therapeutic work.

Appendix C

"Here I Am" Prayer

The intention of this prayer is to "be here now" with God in Prayer.

- Resolve to be in prayer for a specific time (e.g., 5, 10, 15 minutes). Do not answer the phone or allow yourself to be distracted from your goal.
- Be seated and say to yourself, "Here I am seated, doing nothing. I will do nothing for five minutes" (or longer, depending on the time you have set for yourself).
- Begin by noticing your own bodily presence—how your body feels next to the chair; how your feet feel against the floor. Relax your body. Notice your interior feelings.
- Now notice the presence of all that is around you. Say to yourself, "Here I am in the presence of the room (garden, chapel, wherever you are)." Be aware of the furniture, walls, and people in the room. Simply be present and silent in our environment. Relax even more.
- Now say to yourself, "Here I am in the presence of God." Repeat silently to God, "Here I am." Let yourself "be" in the presence of the Holy One until your time goal has been reached.

Adapted by SHP Teresa A. Blythe, *50 Ways to Pray: Practices from Many Traditions and Times* (Nashville: Abingdon Press, 2006), 31-32.

Appendix D

Prayers By Jackie McCullough

Prayer For Deliverance From Bitterness

We came out of the same womb, drank from the same breast, sat on the same lap, yet saw the same world differently. For years I sought to change her, compete with her, and loved to hate her.

We refrained from talking. We grew apart. I refused to forgive. But in praise and worship, You showed me how ugly bitterness made me.

Lord, You are helping me to see my sister as You see her. I thank You, because through prayer, You are helping me to accept my sister's differences, celebrate her victories, recognize her purpose, and work with her downfalls.

Learning to love my sister in this way is liberating. Lord, grant me insight and continue to teach me to be a true friend to a sister I almost lost. God, you are so precious to me. Amen.

MEDITATIONS

Behold, for peace I had great bitterness: but Thou hast in love to my soul delivered it from the pit of corruption: for Thou hast cast all my sin behind Thy back

(Isaiah 38:17).

Let all bitterness, and wrath, and anger, and clamour, and evil speaking, be put away from you, with all malice: and be ye kind one to another, tenderhearted, forgiving one another, even as God for Christ's sake hath forgiven you

(Ephesians 4:31-32).

Beloved, let us love one another: for love is of God; and every one that loveth is born of God, and knoweth God. He that loveth not knoweth not God; for God is love

(I John 4:7-8).

Prayer for Success
by Jackie McCullough

I have tried so hard to accomplish my goals, but they tend to lead me down a dead end street. Father, please help me find the way to make my dreams come true. I do not want to make any more plans or attempt to carry out any former plans, until I hear from You. Are my goals in line with Your goals for me?

Maybe I'm a little too driven to accomplish certain things by a certain time in order to prove my self-worth. I try to make meaningful decisions about my ministry, but it seems to go nowhere. I try to make decision in my career, and again, they go nowhere. I try to make decisions about my personal life (or lack thereof), but they go no further than a thought. What is all of this about?

Lord, help me to focus on Your plan for my life and not to expend energy on my plans, because they are going nowhere. I want Your plan, Your, will, and Your purpose for my life.

How did I ever miss this truth? Teach me to hear You clearly; teach me to follow You closely. Teach me, O Lord, to trust You fully. I will get a journal, Lord, and sit with my Bible open so that I can chart this course with Your Word and through the Holy Spirit. Lift the spirit of anxiety from me and let me learn the power of waiting on "unanswered prayers."

Thank You, Lord, for the peace, because I'm laying down my agenda with a mind to follow Your agenda. I thank You that Your name is a strong tower that I can run into and find refuge. I sense Your presence, and I know that my journey will be different as I set my affections on things above. Thank You for establishing me, settling me, and placing me where You predestined me to be Amen.

Meditations

This book of the law shall not depart out of thy mouth; but thou shalt meditate therein day and night, that thou mayest observe to do according to all that is written therein: for then thou shalt make thy way prosperous, and then thou shalt have good success
(Joshua 1:8).

For I know the thoughts and plans that I have for you, says the Lord, thoughts and plans for welfare and peace not for evil, to give you hope in your final outcome
                    (Jeremiah 29:11 AMP).

But seek (aim at and strive after) first of all His kingdom and His righteousness (His way of doing and being right), and then all these things taken together will be given you besides. So do not worry or be anxious about tomorrow, for tomorrow will have worries and anxieties of its own
                    (Matthew 6:33-34a AMP).

PRAYER FOR INSIGHT
BY JACKIE McCULLOUGH

Lord, it amazes me that things that are not visible strongly influence my life. My pragmatic side pulls me to reason to find the perfect logical explanation; but, I hear a higher call. I feel You tugging at my will, my intellect, and my spirit. This is a time when I must not fear what I cannot explain or what seems impossible or ridiculous. Your Word has become dearer to my soul. The more I struggle to live my life, the more I am gravely impacted by the spiritual realm. But I thank You for more clarity when I read the Bible.

I want to walk in the path of righteousness and freedom. This is my earnest prayer: Illuminate me with Your presence so that I can have Your light and Your life, Yours power and Your peace. Lord, I lift my hands to receive all that You have for me. I open my ears to hear what Your Spirit will say. I lift my eyes to see the path You have determined for me to walk in at this time.

Light, come! Vision, unfold! Understanding, come forth in the name of Jesus.

MEDITATIONS

Who hath ears to hear, let him hear
(Matthew 13:9).

So that thou incline thine ear unto wisdom, and apply thine heart to understanding
(Proverbs 2:2).

The entrance of Thy words giveth light; it giveth understanding unto the simple
(Psalm 19:130).

Prayer for Laughter
by Jackie McCullough

Time and time again, I struggle to laugh. Oh, Lord, why do I find it easier to cry than to take pleasure in the freedom of my joy? Is it that I am so used to suffering that I have forgotten how to enjoy the moment?

I ask You, dear Lord, to reveal the damage that chokes my joy. Help me to acknowledge it, deal with it, and release it. Help me to regain the ability to move readily into hilarity. I know that laughter is good medicine. I know that when I laugh, it lifts the gloom and despair from my spirit. I know You desire for me to have a merry heart. I release the hesitancy and take pleasure in my jolly moments.

My sincere desire is to live this life on a different plane. Pain surpasses the laughter roaring in my belly; my pleasure is suppressed by sorrow. Move the laughter upward and I will bellow without restraint. By faith, I receive my time of celebration in laughter without fear. Thank You, Lord!

Meditations

He will yet fill your mouth with laughter and your lips with shouts of joy
                    (Job 8:21 NIV).

A feast is made for laughter . . .
                    (Ecclesiastes 10:19).

. . . God hath made me to laugh, so that all that hear will laugh with me
                    (Genesis 21:6).

Prayer of Discovery
by Jackie McCullough

I am walking so close to You that each day is a day of new experiences. I started out this day with worship and conversation around Your Word. I didn't expect such a burst of inspiration, such a flood of warm feelings, and such a fullness of Your presence.

Please receive my praise and accept my gratitude, because I am gliding through a journey that broadens my views and opens my heart. Lord, continue to work Your work in me and through me. Continue to lift my vision and guide my expectations.

Oh, what newness; oh, what freshness; and oh, what lightness! I am having a time with You, Lord, which I longed for. Yes! This is how one walks in anointing and power. Glory be to God!

Meditations

And He hath put a new song in my mouth, even praise unto our God: many shall see it, and fear, and shall trust in the Lord.
(Psalm 40:3).

Behold, the former things are come to pass, and new things do I declare: before they spring forth I tell you of them. Sing unto the Lord a new song, and his praise from the end of the earth, ye that go down to the sea, and all that is therein; the isles, and the inhabitants thereof
(Isaiah 42:9-10).

It is of the Lord's mercies that we are not consumed, because His compassions fail not. They are new every morning: great is Thy faithfulness
(Lamentations 3:22-23).

PRAYER FOR EMOTIONAL SPACE
BY JACKIE MCCULLOUGH

Situations and people can torment me so that I need a hiding place. It is so hard at time to find seclusion or downtime, in order to recoup from the blows, disappointments, and disillusionments I encounter periodically. This place is a place of refuge, a place of healing, and a place of quiet rest.

This is what I need every now and then. Help me to know when I must distance myself in order to experience myself in Your divine presence. You love me, You care for me, and You will sustain me. Your arms are strong enough to bear me up in my feeble times; therefore, I cherish the moments that I can be tenderly nurtured and refreshed by You.

There are some friends, family members, and associates who create a toxic atmosphere that seeks to poison my whole existence. I crave for Your presence when the air becomes polluted with hate, anger, envy, jealousy, and unkindness. Show me the escape routes so that I can hide under the shadow of Your wings and be safe. You are my security. O Lord!

MEDITATIONS

Keep me as the apple of the eye, hide me under the shadow of Thy wings, from the wicked that oppress me, from my deadly enemies, who compass me about
(Psalm 17:8-9).

And I said, Oh that I had wings like a dove! For then would I fly away, and be at rest
(Psalm 55:6).

For thou hast been a strength to the poor, a strength to the needy in his distress, a refuge from the storm, a shadow from the heat, when the blast of the terrible ones is as a storm against the wall
(Isaiah 25:4).

PRAYER TO STAND STILL
BY JACKIE MCCULLOUGH

Getting, getting, giving, giving, and moving, moving connote going somewhere in many people's minds. But Lord, I hear in my spirit that I should stand still and see how You are going to bring me out. I could try to fix this problem quickly, but that would abort the opportunity of seeing Your glory.

I must learn to wait for Your glory. Your glory comes when my strength fails. Your glory comes when my solutions peter out. Your glory comes when help from others disappear. I will now stand still and watch Your ingenuity and Your mastery in this situation. Please put a hush in my soul and a calm in my spirit so that I can see Your hand in my life—right now. Thank You, Lord!

MEDITATIONS

And Moses said unto the people, Fear ye not, stand still, and see the salvation of the Lord, which He will show to you today: for the Egyptians whom ye have seen today, ye shall see them again no more for ever
(Exodus 14:13).

He giveth power to the faint and to them that have no might He increaseth strength. Even the youths shall faint and be weary, and the young men shall utterly fall: but they that wait upon the Lord shall renew their strength; they shall mount up with wings as eagles; they shall run, and not be weary; and they shall walk, and not faint
(Isaiah 40:29-31).

And He said unto me, My grace is sufficient for thee: for My strength is made perfect in weakness. Most gladly therefore will I rather glory in my infirmities, that the power of Christ may rest upon me.

Therefore I take pleasure in infirmities, in reproaches, in necessities, in persecutions, in distresses for Christ's sake: for when I am weak, then am I strong
(II Corinthians 12:9-10).

Prayer and Meditations
by Jackie McCullough

I read an article recently about meditation, which is becoming more appealing as a secular exercise. Americans are seeking peace, higher spiritual consciousness, and qualifying personal relationships.

As a Christian, I pray, but church life, home life, and everyday life can keep me so busy that I miss quietness and introspection. I have been taught to pray, worship, praise and fellowship; but I have never been taught to sit still and meditate.

I need to find a place where I stop and think on Your goodness, Your faithfulness, Your kindness, Your wisdom, and Your truth. I need to relax in the warmth of Your arms and draw from the tenderness of Your heart.

Teach me to drink from Your fountain quietly and gaze into Your presence freely. Please let me come away with You into that place of solitude, without fear of stillness, loneliness, or alienation.

In Your presence there is comfort; under the shadow of Your wings is divine protection; and in Your Word is strength and power. Thank You, Lord, for the awareness to stop and think about You.

Meditations

This book of the law shall not depart out of thy mouth; but thou shalt meditate therein day and night, that thou mayest observe to do according to all that is written therein: for then thou shalt make thy way prosperous, and then thou shalt have good success.
(Joshua 1:8).

Thou wilt keep him in perfect peace, whose minds is stayed on Thee: because he trusted in Thee
(Isaiah 26:3).

I was in the Spirit on the Lord's day, and heard behind me a great voice, as of a trumpet
(Revelation 1:10).

And it came to pass, that, when I was come again to Jerusalem, even while I prayed in the temple, I was in a trance
(Acts 22:17)

Prayer For Stewardship
by Jackie McCullough

Generous and bountiful describe Your providential care for me. You have created me with so much life, endowment, and ability. Because You are the Creator, I have a piece of Your power within me. I, however, have neglected to embrace these gifts, cultivate these potentials, and release these talents.

Fear, insecurity, selfishness, rebellion, and ignorance are enemies of the true me. I now see it, and I need Your help to face the worst of me in You so that I can become the best of me through You. Oh Lord, I await this disclosure, and I vow to flow with the discoveries, under Your divine guidance. Thank You, Lord!

MEDITATIONS

So God created man in his own image, in the image of God created He him; male and female created He them. And God blessed them, and God said unto them, be fruitful and multiply, and replenish the earth, and subdue it" and have dominion over the fish of the sea, and over the fowl of the air, and over every living thing that moveth upon the earth
(Genesis 1:27-28).

I wisdom dwell with prudence, and find out knowledge of witty inventions
(Proverbs 8:12).

And unto one he gave five talents, to another two, and to another one; to every man according to his several ability; and straightway took his journey. Then he that had received the five talents went and traded with the same, and made them other five talents.
(Matthew 25:15-16).

Moreover it is required in stewards, that a man be found faithful
(I Corinthians 4:2).

As every man hath received the gift, even so minister the same one to another, as good stewards of the manifold grace of God.
(I Peter 4:10).

Prayer For Mercy
by Jackie McCullough

Lord, daily I receive mercy from Your hand. There isn't a day when I do not see and experience Your goodness. I am the beneficiary of Your compassion, not Your wrath and rejection.

I have done what I wanted to do for most of my life. Now I ready to apply Your forgiveness, dwell under Your shadow, and snuggle up into Your grace. Mercy, Lord!

MEDITATIONS

With the merciful Thou wilt show Thyself merciful, and with the upright man Thou wilt show Thyself upright
(2 Samuel 22:26).

Mercy and truth are met together; righteousness and peace have kissed each other
(Psalm 85:10).

He that followeth after righteousness and mercy findeth life, righteousness, and honour.
(Proverbs 21:21).

He hath shown thee, O man, what is good; and what doth the Lord require of thee, but to do justly, and to love mercy, and to walk humbly with thy God?
(Micah 6:8).

Blessed are the merciful: for they shall obtain mercy
(Matthew 5:7).

Prayer for More Grace
by Jackie McCullough

Every rung on the ladder of life takes me into a new place of challenge and opportunity. These opportunities afford me the privilege of seeing my inner self. I am forced to face myself, without the mask and from under the covers. I have discovered that I cannot make this journey on my own.

I must implore Your grace, Your favor, Your strength, Your courage, and Your wisdom. These are the virtues that will take me through the day-to-day activity, experience, and encounter of my passage. Intelligence, wit, talent, and connection cannot suffice for this place in my life. Your grace, however, is enough. As a matter a fact, it is more than enough. All I want is more and more of Your grace and Your favor for life. Your favor is better than life. Thank You, Lord!

Meditations

For His anger endureth but a moment; in His favour is life: weeping may endure for a night, but joy cometh in the morning.
(Psalm 30:5).

Who art thou, O great mountain? Before Zerubbabel thou shalt become a plain: and he shall bring forth the headstone thereof with shoutings, crying, Grace, grace unto it
(Zechariah 4:7).

And of His fullness have all we received, and Grace for grace. For the law was given by Moses, But grace and truth come by Jesus Christ
(John 1:16-17).

For if by one man's offence death reigned by one; much more they which received abundance of grace and of the gift of righteousness shall reign in life by one, Jesus Christ
(Roman 5:17).

Prayer From a Fluid Place
by Jackie McCullough

I almost slipped these past few days because this place that I am in moves too quickly. Because I am so used to having concrete floors in my life, the fluidity of this faith walk creates momentary anxiety. Humanly speaking, I just want to know that every step will be supported by something that I can depend on. Is that so bad, Lord? Should I feel guilty that I want assurance and consistency? Well, I must say that whether I long for it or not, I still have to depend on You for my direction. Since the bottom line is faith, which is the thing that pleases You and causes You to act, I ask you to give me grace for my faith.

With this needed grace, my faith will hold my feet steady in this period of slippery moves. The places may not change, the changes may not be smooth, and my steps may be awkward; but my heart will be steadily beating with Your grace and Word. I trust You, Lord, for this experience, in Jesus' name. Amen.

MEDITATIONS

Behold, his soul which is lifted up is not upright In him: but the just shall live by his faith
(Habakkuk 2:4).

For we walk by faith, not by sight
(2 Corinthians 5:7).

Now faith is the substance of things hoped for, The evidence of things not seen
(Hebrews 11:1).

But without faith it is impossible to please Him: for he that cometh to God must believe that He is, and that He is a rewarder of them that diligently seek Him
(Hebrews 11:6).

Prayer from a Clear Mind
by Jackie McCullough

Thank You! Thank You! Thank You, Lord! It is amazing how I have blamed everyone else for my challenges, struggles, and failures. It is embarrassing to remember how I have attacked others because I couldn't truly see myself.

All the difficulties that I recently faced were designed to bring me to a central truth in my life. This truth is that I need to change, and it takes pressure to change my character. I thought I was fine and that my faults weren't so bad.

It took You, Lord, to burst open my heart and unveil my eyes so that I could have a clear mind. This test was positioned in my way to carry me closer to Your heart and bring me closer to my greater self. *Thank You, Lord!*

Meditations

Thus my heart was grieved, and I was pricked in my reins. So foolish was I, and ignorant: I was as a beast before Thee. Nevertheless I am continually with Thee: Thou Hast holden me by my right hand. Thou shalt guide me With Thy counsel, and afterward receive me to glory.
(Psalm 73:21-24).

Open Thou mine eyes, that I may Behold wondrous things out of Thy law
(Psalm 119:18).

But blessed are your eyes, for they see: And your ears, for they hear
(Matthew 13:16).

For God, who commanded the light to shine out of darkness, Hath shined in our hearts, to give the light of the knowledge Of the glory of God in the face of Jesus Christ.
(2 Corinthians 4:6).

Prayer from the Soul
by Jackie McCullough

Lord, I feel like I am going through the "valley of the shadow of death" (Ps. 23:24). My soul feels dark and dry. It seems as if I am sinking deeper and deeper into an abysmal state.

I was faced with an unexpected disappointment from someone really close. Their spirit lanced into the fibers of my soul with a reality that was almost unbearable. Pain and torment suctioned my heart and spirit into a tunnel of unending despair.

I see myself failing without the ability to catch myself back. Please, Lord, rescue me, before the day breaks—before the day breaks me! Send help from Heaven, because You are able to keep me from plummeting downward. Shift me to an upward move, and I will praise You as I go higher and higher.

Meditations

For Thou wilt not leave my soul in hell; neither wilt Thou suffer Thine Holy One to see corruption
(Psalm 16:10).

To deliver their soul from death, and to keep them Alive in famine. Our soul waiteth for the Lord: He is our help and our shield
(Psalm 33:19-20).

Why art thou cast down, O my soul? And why art thou disquieted in me? Hope Thou in God" for I shall yet praise Him for the help of His countenance . . . Why art thou cast down, O my soul? And why art thou disquieted Within me? Hope thou in God: for I shall yet praise Him, Who is the health of my countenance, and my God
(Psalm 42:5,11).

Prayer For Daily Lightheartedness
by Jackie McCullough

I want to sing a song that brings back sweet flavor to my soul. How can I live with lightness and freedom, in spite of the burdens and troubles that come to dwell in my space? Lightheartedness is what I want, God, because there is not a problem that You cannot solve and no mountain that You cannot remove.

I know Your power, I want to get to the place where I laugh at the devil and his devices at the onset of the challenge. I want my heart to ring with the melody of joy and my tongue to roll with the glee of happiness. This is the place of true confidence. This life of complete trust. I can be light because I know You will take care of me. Give me this light spirit of the soul. Lord, and my spirit will leap with hilarity. Thank You, Lord—Ha, Ha, Ha!

Meditations

Then he said unto them, Go your way, eat the fat, and drink the sweet, and send portions unto them for whom nothing is prepared: for this day is holy unto our Lord: neither be ye sorry: for the joy of the Lord is your strength
(Nehemiah 8:10).

Then was our mouth filled with laughter, and our Tongue with singing: then said they among the Heathen, The Lord hath done great things for them
(Psalm 126:2).

Rejoice in the Lord always: and again I say, Rejoice
(Philippians 4:4).

Prayer to Appreciate My Gift
By Jackie McCullough

I have gifts that I have taken for granted, Lord. These gifts may not seem grand or pronounced as a musical gift or an athletic gift, yet I have come to appreciate your gifting in me. The gift to be sensitive is a marvelous endowment. It was dormant for many year, because I was so self-centered. It was through adversity and difficulty that I began to see and hear so much with deeper senses.

I hear joy bells in the midst of sorrow, I feel comforted in the midst of grief; and I feel loved in the midst of rejection. Lord, You have done something so marvelous in me, because in time past, I would be so dull of understanding.

This gift to feel, to hear, to see, and to understand beyond the human plane has given me so much life and hope. I may never become a great singer or orator, but I will live with my eyes wide open and my ears highly sensitized to the inspirational unveiling of Your presence. This is truly a divine gift.

Meditations

The law of the Lord is perfect, restoring the soul; the testimony of the lord is sure, making wise the simple. The precepts of the Lord are right, rejoicing the heart; the commandment of the Lord is pure, enlightening the eyes
(Psalm 19:7-8 NAS).

Open my eyes that I may behold wonderful thing from Thy law
(Psalm 119:18 NAS).

For since the beginning of the world men have not heard, nor perceived by the ear, neither hath the eye seen, O God, beside Thee, what He hath prepared for him that waiteth for Him
(Isaiah 64:4).

But as it is written, Eye hath not seen, nor ear heard, neither have entered into the heart of man, the things which God hath prepared for them that love Him
(1 Corinthians 2:9).

Appendix E

Prayer

Dear Lord,

I thank You for this day,
I thank You for my being able to see
and to hear this morning.
I'm blessed because You are
a forgiving God and
an understanding God.
You have done so much for me
and You keep on blessing me.
Forgive me this day for everything
I have done, said or thought
that was not pleasing to you.

I ask now for Your forgiveness.
Please keep me safe
from all danger and harm.
Help me to start this day
with a new attitude and plenty of gratitude.
Let me make the best of each and every day
to clear my mind so that I can hear from You.

Please broaden my mind
that I can accept all things.
Let me not whine and whimper
about things I have no control over.
And give me the best response
when I'm pushed beyond my limits.

I know that when I can't pray,
You listen to my heart.
Continue to use me to do Your will.
Continue to bless me that I may be
a blessing to others.

Keep me strong that I may help the weak.
Keep me uplifted that I may have
words of encouragement for others.

I pray for those that are lost
and can't find their way.
I pray for those that are misjudged
and misunderstood.
I pray for those who
don't know You intimately.
I pray for those that will delete this
without sharing it with others
I pray for those that don't believe.

But I thank You that I believe
that God changes people and
God changes things.
I pray for all my sisters and brothers.
For each and every family member
in their households.

I pray for peace, love and joy
in their homes; that they are out of debt
and all their needs are met.
I pray that every eye that reads this
knows there is no problem, circumstance,
or situation greater than God.
Every battle is in Your hands for You to fight.
I pray that these words be received
into the hearts of every eye that sees it
in Jesus' name. Amen!

—Author Unknown

Appendix F

SANKOFA—(return and fetch it)

"SE wo werE fi na wosan kofa a yenkyi."
It is no taboo to return and fetch it when you forget.
You can always undo your mistakes.

SANKOFA—Go Back and Retrieve

Symbol of Wisdom, Knowledge and the People's Heritage Literal translation: there is nothing wrong with learning from hindsight.

The word SANKOFA is derived from the words SAN (return), KO (go), FA (look, see and take). This symbolizes the Akan's quest for knowledge with the implication that the quest is based on critical examination and intelligent and patient investigation.

The symbol is based on a mythical bird that flies forward with its head turned backwards. This reflects the Akan belief that the past serves as a guide for planning the future, or the wisdom in learning from the past in building the future.

The Akan believe that there must be movement with times but as the forward march proceeds, the gem must be picked from behind and carried forward on the march.

In the Akan military systems, this symbol signified the rearguard, the section on which the survival of the society and the defense of its heritage depended.

Bibliography

Africa Within, *Sankofa*, available from http://www.africawithin.com/studies/sankofa.htm; Internet, accessed 27 October 2008.

Emerson, James. *Forgiveness: Key to the Creative Life.* Bloomington, Indiana: AuthorHouse, 2007.

hooks, bell. *Sister of the Yam: black Woman and Self-Recovery.* Boston, MA: South End Press. 1993.

Jampolsky, Gerald. *Forgiveness: The Greatest Healer of All.* Hillsboro, Oregon: Beyond Words Publishing, Inc., 1999.

McCullough, Jackie. 105 Days of Prayer. Shippensburg, PA: Destiny Image. 2005.

Sullender, Scott R. *Therapy Prayer and Journaling.* San Francisco Theological Seminary.

Author and international speaker Dr. Helen Orme is the founder and Pastor of Shekinah Glory Tabernacle in Renton, Washington. God has gifted Dr. Orme with ministries of deliverance, healing and prophesy. With a genuine passion for the growth and development of God's people in Biblical truth and principles, Dr. Orme is also an Internet talk show host on Blog Talk Radio. Log on to "H.O.M.E. Helen Orme Ministry of Empowerment" at *www.blogtalkradio.com/HOMETalkradio* for dates and times.

Professional Background:

- Doctor of Ministry, San Francisco Theological Seminary, 2009
- Master of Arts in Pastoral Studies, Seattle University, 2007
- Bachelor of Arts, Applied Psychology, City University, Bellevue, 2004
- Bachelor of Arts, Biblical Education (emphasis in Leadership and Policy Studies), Moore-Montgomery College, 2003
- Project Lead Program, United Way of King County, 2003

Additional Ministries of Note:

- Chair of Altar/Prayer Ministry of the Pacific Northwest District Council (PNDC) of the Pentecostal Assemblies of the World
- Served as the Women's Auxiliary Chair for the PNDC
- Founder of J&H Designs providing The Royal Prayer Bolsters®, Miracle Bless Oil, and Prayer Essentials
- Founder and CEO of "The Daughters of Destiny Christian Women's Fellowship" and the Destiny Learning Center in Renton, WA

Past Positions of Note:

- Served as PNDC Registrar for more than 10 years
- Served as licensed national Evangelist of the Pentecostal Assemblies of the World, Inc. for more than 12 years

- Conducted prayer crusades, prayer shut-in services, and retreats
- Established "Front Line Prayer Ministry"
- Former VP, Resolution Committee for the PNDC

"SELF CARE is essential to staying in a Fresh Place."
—*Dr. Helen Orme*

Other Books from Dr. Orme

Divine Touch

Divine Touch is a divinely inspired tool to administer prayer and forgiveness; affirmations, devotional worship phrases, and declaring the "I've Been."

ID: 7613206 *www.lulu.com*

Orme Sermon Delivery Tool

Learn how to organize your sermons notes; seeking before delivering; components of delivery; Helen Orme's Sermon Model, Orme Sermon Delivery Tools and notes.

ISBN:978-0-557-46177-6

Helen Orme Reflections/Testimonials

Reflections from the Self Care Encounter and Soaking

The comments from past participants confirm their divine encounter with God.

"I needed the water to bloom into the flower I really am. I needed the whole weekend for the process to transform me."

"I felt like something was stripped away. I felt 10 to 20 pounds lighter."

"[Now] it is easier to forgive."

"I've gained a positive mode of thinking."

"I'm not bombarded by what goes wrong anymore."

"The majority of my life I've felt like a hand was pressing me down. It's not there anymore. I feel as though I'm standing taller."

"The more I forgave, the bolder I felt in my faith."

"I feel free. I feel like I'm someone else's Goliath instead of someone else being mine. It's not a negative boldness. My self-doubt has taken a back seat."

"I discovered something I've had all the time. Now I can go forth in faith."

"My whole being is now able to move forth in faith."

"I'm walking in the light."

"I'm walking lighter and freer and excited about all of the possibilities."

'I'm looking forward to engaging in self-care."

Edwards Brothers Malloy
Thorofare, NJ USA
October 23, 2014